URBAN IMPACT
LOVE, EQUIP, EMPOWER
BILL HOBBS

urbanpress

Urban Impact: Love, Equip, Empower
by Bill Hobbs
Copyright © 2019 Bill Hobbs

ISBN # 978-1-63360-225-0

Unless otherwise noted, all scripture quotations taken from the Holy Bible, New International Version®, NIV®. Copyright © 1973, 1978, 1984, 2011 by Biblica, Inc.™ Used by permission of Zondervan. All rights reserved worldwide. www.zondervan.com The "NIV" and "New International Version" are trademarks registered in the United States Patent and Trademark Office by Biblica, Inc.

Scripture quotations marked (NASB) are taken from the NEW AMERICAN STANDARD BIBLE®, Copyright© 1960, 1962, 1963, 1968, 1971, 1972, 1973, 1975, 1977, 1995 by The Lockman Foundation. Used by permission.

Scripture quotations marked (Amp) are taken from the AMPLIFIED® BIBLE, Copyright© 1954, 1958, 1962, 1964, 1965, 1987 by the Lockman Foundation Used by Permission. (www.Lockman.org)

Scripture quotations marked (NLT) are taken from THE HOLY BIBLE, NEW LIVING TRANSLATION, Copyright© 1996, 2004, 2007 by Tyndale House Foundation. Used by permission of Tyndale House Publishers, Inc.

Scripture quotations marked (TM) are taken from THE MESSAGE: THE BIBLE IN CONTEMPORARY ENGLISH, Copyright©1993, 1994, 1995, 1996, 2000, 2001, 2002. Used by permission of NavPress Publishing Group

All rights reserved under International Copyright Law. Written permission must be secured from the publisher/author to reproduce, copy, or transmit any part of this book.

For Worldwide Distribution Printed in the U.S.A.

Urban Press
P.O. Box 8881
Pittsburgh, PA 15221-0881 USA
412.646.2780
www.urbanpress.us

DEDICATION

To my darling wife, Kerry, for your selfless and devoted service and support to me and the urban residents that God has called us to serve. Thank you for the tremendous sacrifices you have made at great personal expense. I love you and thank God for you. I could not do what I do without you.

"I knew Bill Hobbs when he was a young golf professional, trying to make a living playing the game. He later discovered, however, that golf should not be his life's total commitment. Instead, Bill found that his commitments to his faith and to golf were much stronger together. Once Bill's self-discovery resulted in a powerful change in his own life, he went to work on how to impact the lives of others—the lives of young people in need. Hopefully, this book and its look at one man's journey will inspire you as Bill Hobbs has inspired the lives of so many others."

**Jack Nicklaus, golf legend,
chairman of the Nicklaus Companies**

FOREWORD

Bill Hobbs is a dear friend and a trusted member of my congregation. I am so proud of his vision and sacrifice to touch the youth in the inner-city of West Palm Beach with the practical love and life-giving message of Jesus Christ. He is an incredible ambassador for Jesus and it is truly an honor to partner prayerfully and financially with him and Urban Youth Impact in their mission to care for the hurting and those who have lost direction in their lives.

Urban Impact: Love, Equip, Empower is an in-depth view of his journey from being a professional golfer to a committed urban worker. I believe Bill's story will inspire and challenge you on many levels. The purity of his ministry is undeniable. I have been blessed and humbled as I've interacted with Bill over the years and heard the many stories of changed lives because of Urban Youth Impact's ministry.

The work they are doing has made an incredible impact on the hearts and lives of those with whom they come in contact. When things have gotten hard, disappointing, or frustrating, they have not pushed back or abandoned their cause. Instead, I've seen them push through strife because they know, firsthand, that nothing they do for Jesus is in vain because He is the one they serve.

God will help Urban Youth Impact to fulfill its calling to love, equip, and empower the urban youth of our region. Seeing His faithfulness, they are committed to bringing light to the darkest of hearts.

As you read this book and as the Holy Spirit stirs your heart, I pray that you will faithfully hold Bill and the Urban Youth Impact team up in prayer. As you pray, please consider how you could volunteer and serve through Urban Youth Impact's various ministry programs.

I am so thankful for Bill and the Urban Youth Impact team. I anticipate hearing more wonderful stories of changed lives in the youth and the community they minister to each day. None of us knows just what God has in store for Urban Youth Impact as they continue to follow God's leading, but I do know the vision keeps unfolding and exciting things are ahead!

Bill, thank you for humbly and obediently sharing your story and your heart. I pray that God will continue to provide a great harvest of souls on your mission field. Thank you for giving Christ Fellowship the opportunity to labor with you. We are so glad you made that long drive from the fairway to the 'hood, and we look forward to seeing how God fulfills His good work through you and your team. May you love, equip, and empower for many more years to come.

Dr. Tom Mullins
Founding Pastor, Christ Fellowship
Palm Beach County, FL

INTRODUCTION

As I wrote this first introduction, our family was on vacation in the mountains of North Carolina. I was recovering from a serious and painful eye surgery to repair a badly torn retina. The doctors told me there was a possibility that I would lose some sight in my left eye. I believed, however, that God would bring complete healing to my physical vision—and He did. There was a deeper work God was doing in my spiritual vision as I embraced His ultimate purpose while suffering from surgical pain.

Yet my pain then, and any pain I have had since, is minor compared to the daily pain in which many urban youth live. They can't get away to North Carolina like I could and do, and they often can't get the medical care they need. I have seen this reality firsthand for the last thirty years.

I decided to write this book to tell my story of what I consider my longest drive, which for me was leaving a career in professional golf to work in the urban community of West Palm Beach. I represent this book now in its second edition because there has never been a greater need for people to understand the plight of our urban poor. I am not a crusader and I have never attempted to make anyone feel guilty as a means to engage their support in my work, but the need and the pain are real.

As I grow older and face my own mortality and as I turn the day-to-day operation on the ministry over to my successor, I am more reflective than I have ever been. I want to solve problems at their root cause, and am not content to build something that will succeed in my lifetime only to fade after I'm gone. I want to make a lasting difference and I want to be faithful to the God who called me to make my longest drive—and not with the driver in my golf bag but with the purpose He assigned to my life.

For someone who is a visionary and driven to do all that God wants in my life, the surgery I mentioned earlier brought me to a sudden halt. Humbled by two weeks of severe headaches and being dependent on my wife for everything, my heart became more sensitive to hurting people because of what God allowed me to go through. Now that I am older, I cry more often, say thank you more frequently, and still drive every day to our facility on Australian Avenue, a few miles away from an urban tragedy that continues to unfold. I know we have made a difference through Urban Youth Impact, but it's not sufficient or fast enough to prevent some pain from happening. I have had to learn that we cannot save the world, only a small piece of it.

Now as I get older, I have to slow down. I bet you may be reading this in agreement, thinking your life is moving too fast and you need to slow the pace. When I do that I'm better able to hear what God is saying to me. He's gotten my attention over the years through my own limitations, and that's why I am adding important information to this book so the UYI story can continue to be told. I hope the next generation will add their own chapters to this story, but that is up to them. My time is coming to an end.

I hope you will laugh and cry at the stories I am about to share in these pages. I especially hope you will read and listen for the voice of God urging you to make a difference in your world. There is plenty of hurt right outside your door and you can play an important role as a source of healing and reconciliation. By the way, all the names have been changed in every story to preserve the confidentiality of the work we do.

As I revise this book, I look out over the mountains of western North Carolina, just like I did with the first edition. I know our Creator God is in control and works all things together for good in His children's lives. As I reflect on this long drive of now more than thirty years of ministry, I also celebrate that we have just about completed our building renovations for the Dream Center facility that you'll read about in later chapters. We have developed partnerships with diverse groups like the City of West Palm Beach, Convoy of Hope and Joyce Meyer Ministries. We have a larger staff than ever before and we are reaching more and more youth in our target area, for God has indeed been good to me and to us.

So enjoy this revised book. I hope you will sit back, quiet your mind, and allow the story of *Urban Impact: Love, Equip, Empower* to sink into your heart.

Bill Hobbs
July 2008 (first edition)
November 2019 (revised edition)

(Special thanks and appreciation to Timeka Motlow, Damaris Medina, and Rozanne N. for editing and great support.)

SECTION 1
THE EARLY YEARS

In this first section, I tell you my life journey that led to the start of Urban Youth Impact, as well as the early years of the ministry and its impact in the local community.

CHAPTER 1
FOR THE LOVE OF GOLF

I was walking out of church years ago with Rachel, my four-year-old daughter (who is now a teenager), when a man and woman stopped me to talk. The man told me that he had become a member at Frenchman's Creek Golf Club in North Palm Beach after I left my position there as head professional in 1983. The man had asked the people at the club why I left and their response was, "Bill became a Jesus freak!" I smiled at the man's comment, delighted to hear his story. In my opinion, being called a "Jesus freak" is one of the greatest compliments I could ever receive. As a former PGA golf professional, my longest drive never took place on the golf course. It happened when I stepped off the golf course and drove into the 'hood. This is my story of that journey.

I grew up in Lockport, New York, a small town near Buffalo, with my parents and sister, Barbara. Lockport's only claim to fame is Bill Miller, the running mate of 1964 presidential nominee Barry Goldwater. I began working in my dad's fish market when I was ten. I got up early every Saturday to work while my friends went out to play and continued to do so until I was eighteen. Though my relationship with my dad was somewhat strained, he instilled in me a strong work ethic. My mother was always a great support to me; she loved and believed in me.

As a young boy, I dreamt about becoming a sports hero. I would imagine myself throwing a touchdown for the New York Giants or hitting a grand slam at Yankee Stadium in the bottom of the ninth to win the game. When I was eight, I fell in love with golf, riding my bike to the golf course every day to practice. I would pretend I was playing with golf legend Jack Nicklaus, making a birdie putt on the eighteenth hole to win the Masters. I never dreamed that one day I would actually play and work with Jack Nicklaus, one of my childhood heroes.

I graduated from high school in 1971 and enrolled at Jacksonville University in Florida. I joined a fraternity and soon began living for my fraternity brothers' approval, giving in to their peer pressure to receive it. The party life at college didn't do much for my grade point average and after two years, I dropped out with a 1.7 GPA. I was eager to get started in the golf business where I knew I could earn some serious money and be somebody important. I moved to Pompano Beach, Florida in 1973 and started working at Boca Teca Country Club parking cars. It was the only job I could find that allowed me to earn money and work on my golf game. I eventually moved into the pro shop and became a professional in 1974.

I played in a lot of tournaments after turning pro. I also began to fulfill the requirements to become a member of the PGA, the Professional Golfers' Association of America. It took me more than four years to complete the process. In the meantime, I fell in love with a tennis pro at a club where I was working. My love for golf and her devotion to tennis worked well for us and we married in 1977. I went on to work as an assistant pro at Amelia Island Plantation, The Everglades Club, Sawgrass Country Club, and Harbor Town Golf Club.

Jack Nicklaus

In 1980, I was thrilled when Frenchman's Creek Golf Club in North Palm Beach, Florida invited me to become their head professional. Frenchman's Creek was a 36-hole facility managed by the Jack Nicklaus Club Management. Here I was, only 27 years-old, and I was going to be working for the greatest name in golf! My wife and I moved to North Palm Beach and I eagerly embraced this new challenge.

During my three years at Frenchman's Creek, I got to know Jack Nicklaus and his family personally. Jack and I played golf together and he helped me with my game, a dream come true for a golf lover and unknown kid from Lockport. I had the privilege of being tutored by Jack's personal teacher, Jack Grout, as well as Gardner Dickinson, Jim Flick, and other professional tour players. When Jack asked me to begin giving golf lessons to his son, Gary, I knew I had arrived as a golf pro. I couldn't believe my good fortune.

This good fortune, however, soon proved to be my downfall. Personal troubles began to simmer under the surface. I was so consumed by my work that my marriage began to suffer. The only thing I cared about was my career and what was good for my image. My wife was somewhere to be found on the tennis court but nowhere to be found in my heart. When 1982 rolled around, I knew my marriage was in serious trouble, and we went through a difficult divorce later that year. It was an emotional death that sent me into depression for months. I thought being single was what I wanted but to my surprise, I was mistaken. After the divorce, I realized I still wasn't happy and found myself very lonely. My love for golf was really only a love for myself and it had left me with nothing at the end of the day.

Little did I suspect then that God would use my failures and subsequent depression to help me find true meaning and purpose in His love and forgiveness. I also didn't realize that I was well on my way to becoming a "Jesus freak"—or that it would be the best thing to ever happen to me.

CHAPTER 2
MEETING JESUS

In December of 1982, I met Julie Cole, an LPGA mini-tour golfer, and she and I became friends. We went out for dinner one night and as we were leaving the restaurant, she gave me her business card. I was intrigued to see Proverbs 3:5-6 on it: "Trust in the Lord with all your heart and lean not on your own understanding; in all your ways acknowledge Him, and He will make your paths straight." Those verses really touched my heart. I had been leaning on my own understanding for most of my life, and it hadn't gotten me very far. In fact, my personal life was a mess.

That night, Julie and I took a walk on the beach and she told me about Jesus and His love for me. I was all ears since I had been longing for something that would bring fulfillment to my life. Perhaps that something was Jesus Christ. The next day, a Sunday, I went to Maranatha Church in Palm Beach Gardens, Florida with a friend of Julie's. The pastor told me that God would forgive my sins if I put my trust in Jesus and gave Him control of my life. I gave my life to Jesus Christ at that moment on January 2, 1983. In the weeks that followed my decision, the Lord began to heal my past pain and reveal His future calling and purpose for my life. My longest drive had begun.

Two significant things happened the first week that I began to follow Jesus. The Sunday that I gave my life to Christ, I returned home after the service and sat on my porch reflecting on this new God thing. As I sat outside, I noticed a beautiful yellow butterfly floating through the air. It came over and landed on a palm tree close to me. Suddenly it flew away, and I silently prayed, "God, if this is all real and you are God, bring that butterfly back to the same spot." At the exact moment I finished saying my prayer, the butterfly flew back to the palm tree and landed on the same spot where it had been before. That was one of my first answers to prayer and helped confirm for me that God was really working in my life. I later learned from reading the Scriptures that God wants us all to have a simple, childlike faith in Him.

The second thing that happened to me was much more dramatic. A week after I had been in church, I was spending time in prayer, asking God about love. I returned to Maranatha Church the following Sunday with a friend and was amazed when the guest pastor, Dr. Arnold Prater, preached on the topic of love. During his message, he said something that has stayed with me to this day: "A bell's not a bell 'til you ring it, a song's not a song 'til you sing it, and the love in your heart was not given to stay, for love was meant to be given away."

After Dr. Prater finished his message, my friend and I made our way toward the back of the sanctuary to leave. We shook hands with Dr. Prater and I'll never forget what happened next. The moment I touched his hand, I saw a bright light shine from his face and felt a warm feeling spread from his hand to mine and touch my heart. I felt blinded for a split second and asked my friend if she had seen what had just happened. She looked at me a little strangely and asked, "What are you talking about?" I can't explain what happened that morning but I believe that God manifested Himself to me through that guest pastor's touch. That split-second moment inspired me to begin seeking God more seriously.

My rising golf career was in for a major disappointment that summer. I accepted a great offer from Jack Nicklaus Club Management to move to Orlando to become the director of golf at Grand Cypress Resort. The day before I was to begin this new job, my boss called me into his office and dropped a bombshell: He didn't believe I was ready for the job and was withdrawing his offer. I felt like I had just been pushed off a cliff! It took me a week to figure out what had really happened. Apparently, I had gotten caught in the middle of some high-powered corporate politics because Club Management had hired a new president. As I look back on it, I know that this upheaval was part of God's plan to increase my trust in Him.

Back Home with Mom and Dad

For the next six months, I struggled to get back on my feet. I couldn't find a job and had no choice but to return to my parents' home in Boca Raton. This was a challenge since I had grown distant from my father. I had judged him over the years for his lack of love and had resented the fact that he didn't spend more time with me when I was a child. After I moved in with my parents, God began to challenge me to honor my parents as the Bible commands. I began to ask for God's forgiveness for my bitter feelings toward my father and God revealed to me that He alone could properly judge my dad's shortcomings:

> The Holy Spirit is the only one in the proper position to criticize, and He alone is able to show what is wrong without hurting and wounding. There is always at least one more fact, which we know nothing about, in every person's situation. I have never met a person I could despair of, or lose all hope for, after discerning what lies in me apart from the grace of God.[1]

The Lord reconciled my father and me and brought great healing to our once fragile relationship.

God did more than bring healing to my relationship with my dad. He also changed what I believed about myself. As a child, I had longed for my dad's approval, which I later transferred to my college friends and golf career. I had worked hard to establish my image in the golf business and earn the approval of those around me. God began to deconstruct this compulsive need to please others and instead, showed me that I was already pleasing to Him. I didn't have to work for God's love; I was just loved and that would never change. As I spent more time reading Scripture and befriending other Christians who accepted me as God did, I finally began to embrace the truth: I was deeply loved, fully pleasing, totally accepted, and complete in Christ. This was all that mattered. As this concept of grace-filled love sunk into my heart, it began to set me free.

The Lord also challenged me with His words in Matthew 16:24: "If anyone desires to come after me, let him deny himself, and take up his cross, and follow me" (NKJV). God asked me if I would deny myself for the cause of Christ, take up my cross, and follow Him. I had a hard time saying yes since my life had revolved around me until then. I didn't want to deny myself, especially since I had spent most of my career building myself up. God helped me understand that this period of time at home was a time of dying to my old self. Unemployed and dependent on my parents, I was learning to trust God and draw closer to Him:

> As long as you maintain your own personal interests and ambitions, you cannot be completely aligned or identified with God's interests. This can only be accomplished by giving up all of your personal plans once and for all, and by allowing God to take you directly into His purpose for the world. Your understanding of your ways must also be surrendered, because they are now the ways of the Lord. I must learn that the purpose of my life belongs to God, not me. God is using me according to His great personal perspective and all He asks of me is that I trust Him. He simply asks me to have absolute faith in Him and His goodness. Self-pity is of the devil, and if I wallow in it I cannot be used by God for His purpose in the world.[2]

Kerry

Living with my parents made me grateful for my family but also lonely for a life companion. I injured my back in 1984 which led to visits to a chiropractor. While at the doctor's office, I met one of his staff: a young woman named Kerry. I shared my newfound faith and love for God with her the first time we met and we became friends. She eventually shared her life story with me and I had the privilege of praying with her to receive Jesus as her Lord and Savior that same year.

Six months later, Kerry and I were married. I was out of the golf business at that time and worked two jobs to pay the bills. I delivered newspapers every day at 3 a.m. and worked at Jordan Marsh, a department store, during the day. This was obviously a far cry from my prestigious golf career with Jack Nicklaus. God humbled me through these circumstances. I certainly wasn't happy with my professional life, but I believed that God was in control and working everything out according to His plan and my good.

In November 1984, God blessed me with an incredible opportunity to return to the world of golf. I accepted the position as head professional at PGA National Golf Club in Palm Beach Gardens, Florida—the home club of the PGA. PGA National had four golf courses and hosted many national events each year. My three years there was a tremendous time of meeting and praying with wonderful people. During my time at the club, I was saddened to learn that one of the members was diagnosed with cancer. He and I became friends and he often visited me in my office where I would pray for him and his health concerns. He eventually passed away from the cancer, but I knew that he had received Christ and was resting in God's promise of eternal life.

Despite the countless opportunities to minister at

the club, there was a longing in my heart to reach out to more people than I was touching at PGA National. Kerry and I developed an empathy for homeless people and began to minister to and feed people God put in our path. We also reached out with the love of Christ to those who were bound by drug addictions. God broke our hearts when we saw people hurting all around us. My desire to touch other people's lives with the love of Jesus that had transformed my own life was overwhelming. I wanted my life to count for eternity and began to sense that God had something great in store for us. God had placed a burden for the poor in our hearts and we soon found ourselves immersed in a whole new world, far from the fairways and greens that had been such an important part of my life. My longest drive continued.

CHAPTER 3
FROM THE FAIRWAY TO THE 'HOOD

I knew the Lord was redirecting my life and, after much prayer and counsel, sensed that God wanted me to surrender my golf career and its image of success to Him. He spoke to me through the story of Abraham and his son, Isaac, found in Genesis 22. Just as God asked Abraham to sacrifice his son, I believed God was asking me to sacrifice the golf career I loved and turn it over it to Him:

> "Later on God tested Abraham's faith and obedience. 'Abraham!' God called. 'Yes," he replied. 'Here I am.' 'Take your son, your only son—yes, Isaac, whom you love so much—and go to the land of Moriah. Sacrifice him there as a burnt offering on one of the mountains, which I will point out to you'" (Genesis 22:1-2).

God also spoke to me at that time through a quote from C. G. Trumbull:

> And from that day to this, men have been learning that when, at God's voice, they surrender up to Him the one thing above all else that was

dearest to their very hearts, that same thing is returned to them by Him a thousand times over. Abraham gives up his one and only son, at God's call, and with this disappears all his hopes for the boy's life and manhood, and for a noble family bearing his name. But the boy is restored; the family becomes as the stars and sands in number, and out of it, in the fullness of time, appears Jesus Christ.

That is just the way God meets every real sacrifice of every child of His. We surrender all and accept poverty; and He sends wealth. We renounce a rich field of service; He sends us a richer one than we had dared to dream of. We give up all our cherished hopes, and die unto self; He sends us the life more abundant and tingling joy. And the crown of it all is our Jesus Christ. For we can never know the fullness of the life that is in Christ until we have made Abraham's supreme sacrifice. The earthly founder of the family of Christ must commence by losing himself and his only son, just as the Heavenly Founder of that family did. We cannot be members of that family with the full privileges and joys of membership upon any other basis.[3]

My desire to serve God continued to grow, as did my desire to minister to broken people so I became involved with Maranatha Church's healing ministry. Whenever Kerry and I were out driving, we were always drawn to help the homeless people we saw on the streets. One night, we picked up a homeless man and brought him to our home at PGA National where he ate, bathed, and spent the night. Kerry spent the next day helping him find work and after he went on his way, we felt like we had done exactly what God had wanted us to do. Years later, we received a call in the middle of the night from this same man. He left a simple message on our answering machine: "I'm the guy you helped. Thanks very much."

After three great years at PGA National Golf Club, I was feeling restless and began to sense that change was coming. The management of the club changed and I got a new boss, and it soon became obvious that he wanted to hire his own person to take over my position. I resigned from PGA National in 1987 and started a professional golf school with Dan Pasquariello, a longtime friend and fellow golf professional.

In the spring of 1988, I began a three-day fast with a fellow church member in order to seek God's will, asking Him to open the door He wanted me to walk through. I wanted His will to be done. At the end of the three-day fast, Dan informed me that he had accepted a new job and was moving to Hawaii. Within a few days, the golf course where we worked was sold and I was out of work.

The following week, a good friend from Youth for Christ where I was volunteering, called to ask if I would be interested in coming on staff. Youth for Christ wanted to begin a youth guidance program for juvenile delinquents and incarcerated youth. It seemed like a good match for the burden the Lord had placed in my heart.

As Kerry and I prayed about this transition, we knew

God was moving us but also sensed that it was going to be a difficult transition. Moving from the golf business with its comfortable lifestyle into full-time ministry would be a major step, but I sensed God's peace and knew we had to follow our Lord in faith. Within a matter of weeks, Youth for Christ offered me a position to lead their youth guidance program. My starting salary was $16,000 a year—half of which I had to raise. This was a huge drop from my previous salary as head professional with PGA National. Nonetheless, I was excited because I believed this was God's will.

Joining Youth for Christ resulted in a major lifestyle change for Kerry and me. We moved into a two-bedroom apartment and drastically reduced our budget. Kerry worked two jobs—earning more than I did, of course—and walked to work every day because we only had one car. A former staff member from PGA National learned of our need for another car and gave us a 1968 Pontiac Bonneville for Kerry to drive. We were thankful for God's provision and maintained a sense of humor when we had to drill holes in the floorboard because the backseat flooded every time it rained. Sometimes, the tail lights would fall out and I would tell Kerry, "Honey, don't worry about it. I'll put some duct tape on them until God provides something else." It was a wonderful and hilarious time, but it wasn't easy.

Ava

During my first week on staff with Youth for Christ, I went to the Palm Beach County Juvenile Detention Center. I had learned that the nurse there was a Christian and that she wanted to meet with me. After I arrived, the nurse made her request. "Bill," she began, "I need you to meet with Ava. She's thirteen and has been here a week. We told her today that she's HIV-positive and pregnant." This 13-year-old had been selling herself on the streets to satisfy her drug addiction.

As I walked into the dorm room where Ava lived, I came face to face with a thin girl with bleached blond hair and sunken eyes that revealed a hopeless heart. I proceeded to share God's message of love and hope with her and she seemed interested. As we talked about God's love and the hope that we have in Jesus, I prayed with Ava to receive Christ. After leaving the detention center that day, I continued to pray for Ava and her baby. When her baby was born, she learned that the baby was HIV-negative. It was a miracle.

Unfortunately, Ava returned to the streets since she had little family support. Her father was dead and her mother was out of the picture, so Ava aimlessly roamed the streets. Kerry and I ministered to Ava for the next six years. I didn't know if our times with her were making any difference, but God encouraged me to be faithful in sharing His love with this troubled young woman.

After a seven-year period of not hearing from Ava, I received a phone call from her in 2007. She wanted to visit me at the Urban Youth Impact office. I was eager to see if Ava had changed and we embraced the moment she came into my office. I was overjoyed to learn that she was drug-free and employed. We reminisced about our first meeting at the detention center and our long friendship, the difficult memories bringing tears to our eyes. She said,

"Mr. Bill, you said to me many years ago that if I believed in Jesus, I would never die. I will never forget that message of hope you gave me."

Tamarind Avenue

My ministry with Youth for Christ continued as I met regularly with young men and women who were incarcerated in the juvenile detention center. As I looked into their eyes, listened to their stories, and prayed with them, I sensed a tremendous burden and brokenness in these youth. I was alarmed by the number of fatherless African American children who were in the detention center. Whenever I asked them where their fathers were, they often glared at the floor and stiffened their bodies in response, revealing their feelings of rejection and hatred for the fathers who had abandoned them. Coming from a protected, suburban background, I was unaware that so many African American youth were living without the support of their dads. Some didn't even know their fathers at all. Whenever I met with these kids, I was reminded of Psalm 68:5: "A father to the fatherless, of defender of widows, is God in His holy dwelling." sensed that God was calling me to be a faithful, loving, consistent father-figure in a community ravaged by fatherlessness.

As my ministry to the youth in the detention center grew, it became evident to me that I needed to work directly in the community and get involved with the boys and girls at an early age before they got into serious trouble and hardened their hearts. I began a weekly sports outreach in the Tamarind Avenue corridor of West Palm Beach, which turned out to be a great draw for the young men in the neighborhood. The outreach began simply. I would load up my car with sports equipment, find an empty lot in the inner-city, and invite the neighborhood boys to play ball. Within a few weeks, about forty boys were coming together once a week to play football and basketball, eat a meal, and hear the gospel.

Tamarind Avenue is notorious for having the highest number of violent crimes in Palm Beach County. At that time, very few social service agencies or churches were reaching out to that community because of its violent crime rate. Though this was a legitimate concern for me as an outsider, I knew that this was where God wanted me to be and that building relationships with the youth was what He wanted me to do. I could think of no better way to father the fatherless children than to be with them on their own turf.

Marcus

Another special boy who attended the sports outreach was Marcus, a star football player at a local high school. He played football with us on Thursday nights and his presence always drew more kids since many of them looked up to him. It frustrated me that Marcus often slipped out before I shared the gospel with the group. On a Friday that followed one of our regular gatherings, I received a phone call from one of Marcus' friends. It was a call I wish I hadn't received, and a call I will never forget.

His friend called to tell me what had happened after our outreach the night before. Marcus had returned home that night to play cards with his friends and when he won the game, one of his friends became angry. The two young men went outside and Marcus wrestled his friend to the ground, pinning him down. After they wrestled, Marcus followed his friend back into the house. Upon entering the front door, his friend smashed Marcus in the head with a baseball bat, killing him. Marcus was eighteen.

I grieved deeply over Marcus' death, especially since I didn't know if he had ever received Christ. Even so, I fervently prayed that God would use this tragedy to reach others. We took many of the kids from the sports outreach to his funeral where the gospel was shared. Many of the kids opened their hearts to receive Christ at Marcus' service, and it was an important reminder for me that none of us know how long we have left here on earth; each day could be our last. Perhaps this is why Joshua declared, "Choose *today* whom you will serve."[4]

As the weekly sports outreach continued, I began to take the boys camping in the summer, giving them the opportunity to see another world outside the inner-city. We canoed, walked together for miles through the woods, and participated in team-building activities that cultivated leadership skills. The boys and I also took prison tours during the camp trips that were always an eye-opening experience for us all.

One summer, I took nine first-time offenders on a prison tour. I will never forget the looks on their faces during our visit to Marion Correctional Institution in Lowell, Florida, where the reality of prison life stared them right in the face. One of the inmates lamented that he had never listened to his parents, teachers, or friends who tried to help him. He had ignored their attempts to help and did what he wanted. His selfish attitude led to his arrest and imprisonment where he could no longer make his own choices. Instead, the prison system dictated every aspect of his life.

After the tour ended, I wondered how this shocking experience had affected the boys. One declared, "I will never go back there again." We sat around the campfire that evening and I challenged the young men to make the most important decision they could ever make. I assured them that God had a plan for their lives, one to prosper them and give them hope, but that the choice was up to them. By the grace of God, five of the boys came forward and hammered a nail into a wooden cross to symbolize their commitment to Jesus Christ. I praised God for the choice they made to follow Jesus and not their own desires.

Reggie and Devontae

One young man who made that decision was Reggie. I met Reggie when he was 16 years old and he attended our weekly sports outreach. He was only five when he ran away from home for the first time, desperate to escape his family. His stepfather smoked crack, sold the family's Christmas gifts to buy drugs, and beat Reggie and his mother with a belt. All he and his siblings could do was cry.

Thankfully, Reggie's living situation changed. He eventually moved in with his grandmother while his siblings were placed in the state's custody. Reggie gave his life to Jesus at one of our summer camps and went on to become the first person in his family to graduate from high school. Today, Reggie actually works for Urban Youth Impact, and I am always blessed to see his progress and hear his testimony as he raises his own family. You will read more about his story in the next updated section.

In addition to the weekly sports outreach and the summer camping, I started a creative monthly outreach called Friday Night Jam. I approached a local school to ask if we could use its gym and the principal agreed, but insisted that we ensure a police presence during every outreach. Friday Night Jam drew about 250 kids each month where Christian artists performed, Christian athletes shared their testimonies and the gospel, and we provided lots of free pizza. Even though a few fights broke out, we still saw many kids accept Christ.

One of the boys who attended Friday Night Jam was Devontae, an 11-year-old boy living with his mother and older brother. His father was in jail and Devontae hadn't seen him since he was two. At Christmas time, Kerry and I delivered gifts to Devontae and his brother. While in their home, Kerry and I were deeply moved by the condition in which Devontae's family lived. Their bare Christmas tree had been placed in a rubber trashcan and propped up in the corner of their kitchen. Devontae was happy to receive our gifts and as we were leaving, he hung the two candy canes we had just given him on the naked Christmas tree. Two weeks later, Devontae's mother called and asked me to come over because Devontae had run away from home. Kerry and I returned to their home to talk and pray with her and thankfully, he returned home three days later.

At one of our Friday Night Jams, I listened as former NFL player Art Moore challenged the youth to come forward and make a stand for Christ. At first, only one small boy came forward and stood alone. That boy was

Devontae. By the end of the night, however, 39 youth had received Jesus Christ as their Lord and Savior. More than 1,000 youth attended a total of seven Friday Night Jams, and our staff prayed with and counseled 171 kids who made commitments to Christ. God was touching dozens of young hearts and the ministry was overwhelming. I was disappointed that the local churches who knew about the outreach didn't get more involved to help us disciple the kids. I knew that the notoriety of the neighborhood kept many away, so I prayed that God would bring us more help in His time and way.

I was elated to see what God was doing through my initial efforts to father the fatherless in the inner-city of West Palm Beach. What began as a small weekly sports outreach expanded to our summer camping trips, prison tours, Friday Night Jams, and other evangelistic outreaches where professional athletes and rap artists shared the gospel. As I reflected on how God had grown our little ministry in the inner-city, it became apparent to me that He wanted to use me as an instrument of His love and light, one child at a time. I sensed that this would be the only way to effectively father the hundreds of other Reggies and Devontaes living along Tamarind Avenue.

But how could I effectively do this? How could I impact the lives of these young men and women? I knew it would require more than once-a-week meetings and calls for salvations. Though I didn't have the expertise, I did have the heart, and I have found that, if we are willing, God will lead us to the information, the people, and the resources to accomplish what He puts in our hearts to do. That was the case with me, and in the days and years to come, God gave me more wisdom and resources to make the longest, straightest, best drive I have ever made—from the fairway to the 'hood.

CHAPTER 4
A FATHER TO THE FATHERLESS

In David Blakenhorn's book, *Fatherless America*, he exhorts Americans to confront our most urgent social problem: fatherlessness. He states that more than half of American children spend at least half of their childhood without a father in the home. Blankenhorn argues that, in the face of teenage pregnancy, crime, violence against women, educational failure, and child poverty, no social trend of our generation is more dangerous than fatherlessness. It weakens families, harms children, causes or aggravates our worst social problems, and makes individual adult happiness harder to achieve.[5]

Fatherlessness is particularly rampant in the African-American community and "we deceive ourselves if we deny that there is a crisis among black families. Roughly seventy percent of black babies are born each year to single mothers. In 1950, five out of every six black children were born into a two-parent home. Today, that number is less than two out of six. In poor communities, that number is still low."[6]

I still had no doubt that God wanted to use me to be a father to fatherless children and had been preparing me to take on that role for quite some time. Over the years, I had always empathized with the children who didn't know where their daddies were. I learned that this strong desire to love the abandoned children and the widows (single mothers) in the inner-city was rooted in Scripture:

- "A father to the fatherless, a defender of widows, is God in His holy dwelling" (Psalm 68:5).
- "He defends the cause of the fatherless and the widow and loves the alien, giving him food and clothing" (Deuteronomy 10:18).
- "Do not deprive the alien or the fatherless of justice or take the cloak of the widow as a pledge" (Deuteronomy 24:17).
- "Learn to do right! Seek justice, encourage the oppressed. Defend the cause of the fatherless, and plead the case of the widow" (Isaiah 1:17).

God's heart for the fatherless, which is so evident in Scripture, became a special calling for Kerry and me as I continued in my ministry, first with Youth for Christ and then with Urban Youth Impact. Every child I've met over the years has been precious to me, and I have already shared some of their stories with you, but a few boys in particular have truly become my sons.

An Instrument of God's Love

I met Lucas when he was court-ordered to attend

a Youth for Christ program I was running. His father was in jail and his mother was battling a drug addiction. At the tender age of 11, Lucas had already had run-ins with the law while hanging out on the streets, getting into fights, and destroying property. Lucas and I developed a close relationship while he completed community service hours at the Youth for Christ center. In 1991, he accepted Christ and made a commitment to follow Him. That summer, he put his newfound faith into action by attending DC '91, a conference on student evangelism. After his conversion, Lucas told me that he no longer held hatred and anger in his heart. All he wanted to do was love people.

Kerry and I took Lucas on a mission trip to the Dominican Republic in the summer of 1992. He was the only inner-city kid in our group. Lucas's heart was deeply touched when he saw the Dominican orphans living in worse conditions than any he had seen in the inner-city. The following summer, the three of us returned to the Dominican Republic with a group of thirty-five people. Lucas stayed at the orphanage again and loved the kids more than ever. I was overjoyed at the marvelous transformation God had made in his life by transforming him from an inner-city delinquent to an instrument of God's love.

Unfortunately, I also learned that being a father to the fatherless did not come without its heartaches and challenges. When Lucas was seventeen, he was walking down the street one night with two of his friends. One of the guys started talking about robbing an ATM at a nearby bank and Lucas went along with them, never considering the consequences. He and his friends were arrested that night and charged with strong-armed robbery, kidnapping, and grand theft auto. Because Lucas didn't have enough strength to walk away from his friends, his life changed forever.

Several of Lucas's supporters and I attended the hearing for his final sentencing. The judge couldn't believe that a young man who had so much support could end up in such a sorry situation. By God's grace, Lucas received a light sentence of four years in a youth offender's program, where I visited him as often as I could. After he was released, Lucas returned to West Palm Beach. He is now working full-time and stays involved with his family.

God's Special Gift

I'll never forget the first time I saw Lucas's cousin, Michael. Every Thursday night I would drive the Youth for Christ van through the neighborhood, picking up kids to take them to the weekly sports outreach. One day, little Michael was standing at one of the pick-up spots with a wide grin on his face, but he wasn't old enough to join us. When Michael turned ten, I finally allowed him in the van. He was thrilled to play sports every week and go camping with us to Ocala National Forest near Gainesville, Florida. He stayed close by my side as we canoed and hiked during the day, and he and four other boys shared a tent with me at night.

Michael never knew his father and his mother was living on the streets, addicted to crack cocaine. She used drugs while she was pregnant with Michael, which affected his mental development. Without his parents in the picture, he often found himself living in abusive situations and struggled with perpetual fear.

Michael became a son to Kerry and me. We allowed him to spend the night at our home where he helped us cook breakfast. He began to call us "Dad" and "Mom." Michael is a high school graduate and now in his thirties, but every year (since he was 10), we take him out to celebrate his birthday. When he can, he helps with UYI's weekly outreach ministry sharing the love of Jesus with the kids. Despite the pain he has endured, Michael still has that same grin I saw the first time we met. He is God's special gift to us and he loves Jesus today more than ever.

Driven to Succeed

I met Rickie when he was 16 years old. He loved coming to our weekly sports outreach to play football and went camping with us, too. During one camping trip, Kerry and I sat around the campfire with Rickie and fourteen other boys and shared the gospel with them. Rickie came forward, knelt at the wooden cross we brought with us, and prayed with me to receive Christ.

There was something special about Rickie. He had an inner drive that many of the other boys lacked. He received a scholarship through Urban Youth Impact to attend Northfield Mount Hermon School in Massachusetts for a year before being accepted to Clemson University in South Carolina. Sadly, both of Rickie's parents passed away during his four years at Clemson, so Kerry and I included him in our growing family of "adopted" sons. We encouraged and loved him through his senior year and were so proud to see him walk across the stage at his graduation, having earned a degree in wildlife biology. Rickie always said that he wanted to come back and work with the ministry that had touched his life, so he spent three years working as a tutor in UYI's after school program. Rickie has since moved back to South Carolina and is working there full-time.

Isaiah

When Isaiah was born, his mom and dad forfeited their parental rights so Grandma took over and they moved down to the Tamarind Avenue community. They moved into Dunbar Housing Projects, which was one of the worst places in the area. Isaiah started coming to our program when he was 13 or 14 years old and by then, Grandma was in a wheelchair. It was amazing to see her commitment to raise him. She would come over every other week and say, "Mr. Bill, Isaiah has bad friends and needs your help." We were glad to take under our wing and began to mentor him.

As we did, we found out he wanted to be a lawyer. We connected him when he was 16 with a local lawyer who was a friend of ours, and he started mentoring Isaiah. Isaiah was a good student and Grandma stayed on him. He graduated high school and went to Williams College. Then he began to work during his summer breaks for Craig Goldenfarb in Palm Beach County. Craig was impressed with Isaiah, to the point that he came to us and said he wanted to meet UYI and Bill Hobbs. When it came time for Isaiah to graduate from college, Craig came and said he wanted to do a scholarship in honor of Isaiah and therefore every year about $10,000 is given away in his name. At the same time, Isaiah got a full scholarship to the University of Notre Dame Law School, from which he graduated in

2019. Isaiah went from the ghetto to the courtroom. It's an amazing story.

Isaiah has spoken at our annual gala and he also comes and talks to our youth at UYI. His heart is to give back. When I asked him what he wanted to do after he graduated, he said he really wanted to help the underprivileged gain justice. He wants to see their story be told and to have fair representation when they get into trouble.

James

James is a young man who grew up in a single-parent home. He came to our Reframe work program, which was for those aged 16 and up, in which we focused on academic and job prep and training. James was an exceptional student and was coached through Reframe. We were able to allow him to attend Reframe on a scholarship where he was fast-tracked trained for computer coding. He fell in love with electronics and technology, and was awarded the Emanuel McMiller Scholarship and is attending Florida State University where he is studying computer technology, and began attending when he was 17 years old.

There were so many things we were learning, but so much yet to learn. One thing was clear: These young men and women had names, each one had a story, and our job was to learn their names and listen to their stories. They were stories of abandonment and disappointment, of pain and sorrow, of alienation and suffering. Kerry and I, along with the team God began to give us, found ways to listen and bring God's healing power and love to each young life.

Even though our skin had less pigment than the majority of kids to whom we ministered, we quickly learned we could still be agents of God's healing and reconciliation. We learned people didn't care how much we knew until they knew how much we cared. Once they knew we cared, we could bring what we knew about the love of Christ into their battered young lives. What's more, we found that this love had the capacity and ability to overflow into the families and neighbors of each young person.

Becoming a father to these fatherless children was not without our own personal pain, for Kerry and I were unable to have children of our own. While we ached and yearned to have our own family, God brought us all the children we could handle. We were called to minister to those who didn't look like us but had the same needs that we did. We learned to look past our own pain to embrace and feel the pain of others.

As our hearts grew and expanded, so did our vision for the inner-city. With a greater vision came a need for greater faith, but we believed that no matter how big our dream was, God's was always bigger. In the days to come, we would be amazed and humbled by how God would use us.

CHAPTER 5
OUR VISION, GOD'S FAITHFULNESS

After eight years on staff with Youth for Christ, I learned that inner-city youth living in poverty faced complex needs that required a comprehensive, holistic response. Oftentimes, the options they had were limited." People living in poverty look at a situation and cannot say, 'Well, I could pursue A, B, or C. Which one makes the most sense? Which would turn out best for me and my family?' No, under the circumstances, there is only choice A. That is the reality of poverty."[7]

The kids' need for salvation was obviously critical, but if they couldn't read, obtain employment, buy food, or secure stable housing, how could they reach their full potential? The Lord was challenging me to step out in faith and leave Youth for Christ so I could focus all my energy on being a father to the fatherless through my own organization.

In 1997, Urban Youth Impact was born. Kerry and I started UYI in an 800 square-foot office with one computer, a donated van from Youth for Christ, and the 40 boys who had been attending our weekly sports outreach. Kerry began working in the office full-time and spent endless hours setting up the office and administrative aspects of the ministry. I was proud to see my wife work so hard to lay the foundation for our communications, mailings, and donor recruitment. She was a tremendous support and encouragement to me then and still is today, although her role has changed and she is less involved in the day-to-day ministry.

Our budget that first year was $60,000 thanks to the support of a friend and fellow minister, Reverend Dwight Stevens, who believed in our work. We also shared our tiny office with Pathway of Life Fellowship Church and a dear friend, Pastor Carlton Gant, which allowed us to save our resources and have a greater impact.

LEE

Luke 2:52 states, "Jesus grew in wisdom and stature, and in favor with God and men." Just as Jesus grew mentally, physically, spiritually, and socially, we wanted to help the kids grow in every way so they could fulfill their God-given potential. We crafted a mission statement to capture the heart of our work: loving, equipping, and empowering inner-city youth and their families to fulfill their God-given purpose. Today, we refer to our mission statement as LEE and everyone on staff knows exactly what we mean.

We felt compelled to love because Scripture commands us to love. Ephesians 5:1-2 states, "Be imitators of God, therefore, as dearly loved children, and live a life of love just as Christ loved us and gave himself up for us as a fragrant offering and sacrifice to God." First Corinthians 13, the famous love chapter in the Bible, tells us that love bears all things, believes all things, hopes all things, and endures all things. We wanted to love the kids in the community with that kind of genuine love.

We also wanted to equip the kids wholly and develop them mentally, physically, spiritually, and socially. After all, Jesus grew in wisdom and stature and in favor with God and men (see Luke 2:52). He grew holistically and we wanted to help meet the spiritual and natural needs of the youth.

In addition to loving and equipping, we had a strong desire to empower the kids so they could fulfill their God-given purpose. Many of the youth had never heard God's promise for their lives: "For I know the plans I have for you," declares the Lord. "Plans to prosper you and not to harm you, plans to give you a hope and a future" (Jeremiah 29:11). We wanted the kids to hear this promise, believe in it, and know they could attain it for themselves.

LEE became our mission statement and we felt it was more important than ever to know what we were doing and why we were doing it. We began studying the Bible to read and reread some important passages that revealed God's character as a father and a protector of the poor:

> "Though my father and mother forsake me, the Lord will receive me" (Psalm 27:10).
>
> "A father to the fatherless, a defender of widows, is God in His holy dwelling" (Psalm 68:5).
>
> Then these righteous ones will reply, "Lord,

when did we ever see you hungry and feed you? Or thirsty and give you something to drink? Or a stranger and show you hospitality? Or naked and give you clothing? When did we ever see you sick or in prison, and visit you?" And the King will tell them, "I assure you, when you did it to one of the least of these my brothers and sisters, you were doing it to me!" (Matthew 25:37-40).

Most importantly, in the four gospels it was evident that Jesus loved the poor and ministered in many ways just to them:

> [Jesus]defined his primary mandate, his 'job description,' in his first public opportunity to preach in his hometown synagogue in Nazareth. Of all the scriptures he could have chosen as his text, he selected the surprising passage of Isaiah 61:12: 'The Spirit of the Sovereign Lord is on me, because the Lord has anointed me to preach good news to the poor. He has sent me to bind up the brokenhearted, to proclaim freedom for the captives and release from darkness for the prisoners, to proclaim the year of the Lord's favor.' Then he dropped his bombshell: 'Today this scripture is fulfilled in your hearing' (Luke 4:21). Having thus declared his mission and identity, he immediately made clear his heart for the poor, the neglected, and the marginalized.[8]

Kerry and I also dreamed of establishing a Christ-centered

outreach facility where we could minister to the youth. We began to put together a multi-faceted vision for the ministry, and I'm amazed how some of those dreams have come true so quickly! Keep in mind that some of our vision has changed as we gained experience and made mistakes, but that original vision included:

1. The Dream Center, a Christ-centered outreach facility;
2. The Urban Leadership Institute, which provides training for staff and community members;
3. Satellite ministry centers throughout Palm Beach County;
4. Bow Down, a worship service relevant to inner-city youth and their families;
5. A private Christian school for inner-city youth;
6. Impact Coffee Company, a business to provide jobs for our youth and income for UYI.

As much as Kerry and I had a vision for what God was going to do, it became clear that His preparation work in us was a key priority. Hebrews 6:12b instructs us "to imitate those who through faith and patience inherit what has been promised." God promised to provide for us and we had seen His provision throughout my eight years on staff with Youth for Christ. I didn't have any shortage of faith, but patience was the part that challenged me the most.

According to author and pastor Frank Damazio, "[In the Time Test], by all outward appearances, God does not seem to be fulfilling the word He gave a leader in the past. The Time Test tries a leader's patience, forcing him to trust God to fulfill His call and ministry in His own time and way."[9] I experienced a time test from God like never before. I wanted to establish our outreach center right away, but God reminded me that it would all happen in His time and for His glory. He wanted me to simply trust Him and not lean on my own understanding.

God stretched us greatly during those first few years. We couldn't afford to take any vacation time or hire additional staff, and God used that hard period to test us. Would we continue to follow Him, maintain pure motives, and surrender to His will even when it got tough? Once again I quote Frank Damazio:

> God has a very special and unique preparation for each one of His leaders. Testing of that preparation is the final step, and it often comes in the middle of the most ministry activity. Why do you have to be tested? Doesn't God know if you're ready to minister? Of course He does. But you need to know it, too. The very act of testing is itself the final preparation, and can drive you into a deeper relationship with God as nothing else can.[10]

Jesus said, "If anyone desires to come after Me, let him deny himself, and take up his cross, and follow Me" (Matthew 16:24 NKJV). Getting Urban Youth Impact off the ground required that we deny ourselves daily, accept the challenges of starting a ministry from scratch, and surrender to God all our hopes and dreams for the ministry.

One of the first challenges we faced was expanding our outreach to include the girls in the community. A sports outreach wasn't going to cut it with them. Since Kerry was busy in the office, I needed to find other women who could begin a new outreach and build relationships with the girls. The first two women I approached for help were Yvonne Cooper and Sherry Scott, who was on our advisory board.

As a nurse and former lawyer, Sherry was hesitant to accept the offer, but felt challenged to get more involved. After spending time in prayer, Sherry returned to me and said, "I'm ready. I don't know what I'm doing, but I'm ready for God to use me." Soon after, Sherry started a girl's outreach. She and the girls met on a regular basis for Bible study along with life skills and etiquette lessons. I was excited to see our ministry to the girls in the inner-city begin to take shape. Yvonne also stepped right in because she was working as a nurse in the Palm Beach County Detention Center and developed empathy for the girls there. Both women have faithfully served with UYI for many years.

The PARK Center

Though I had the feeling our outreach facility wouldn't become a reality until later, I often found myself driving through the inner-city of West Palm Beach looking for warehouses or empty buildings that we could possibly call home. Just as I had suspected, all possible leads only led to dead ends. Since we were short on money, we decided to partner with a local school in 1998 to give us a place to meet with the kids. We raised money to rent a room at the school and called it the PARK Center, which stood for Positive Atmosphere Reaching Kids. We kept the PARK Center open six evenings a week.

The school was in an ideal location, right across the street from Dunbar Village, one of the oldest housing projects in West Palm Beach. The Lord provided more than $20,000 so we could install a first-class sound system, pool tables, and an air hockey table. We filled the walls with posters of athletes, put in a little basketball hoop, and kept the sodas and chips well-stocked. More than 75 youth regularly attended the PARK Center during our first year there. We also began to hold weekly outreaches at the PARK Center where we shared the gospel, studied the Bible, and counseled kids one-on-one.

We were in one of the most dangerous parts of the city every night, which created new challenges for us. Young drug dealers and thugs often stopped by the PARK Center to play pool or hang out and I wasn't sure how to safely include these potentially troublesome visitors. They needed a positive place to hang out in the evenings just like any other kid in the inner-city, but I also knew that many of these kids just wanted to cause trouble. One night we heard a loud boom that sounded like an exploding bomb and I later learned that a young man had set off a chemical bomb right outside our front door. The school found out too, and due to liability issues and other fears, asked us to close the PARK Center a few months later.

Though we experienced this disappointing setback, God still revealed His faithfulness in a tough time. Kerry and I drove an old station wagon at the time and with 125,000 miles on it, the car had definitely seen better days.

Though the car repeatedly broke down on us, we needed it for personal use and to transport kids involved in our outreach. I recall loading thirteen kids into the wagon at one time and Kerry and I always laugh when we remember the care we took to put plastic seat covers with little bumps over all of the seats. One day the station wagon broke down for good and I was amazed when one of our board members bought another station wagon for us that was almost brand new. God's faithfulness kept me going, especially when I grew discouraged over the closing of the PARK Center. If God could faithfully provide our transportation needs, surely He could provide another building.

Partnerships

Still disappointed but believing in God's ability to provide, I returned to the drawing board, driving through the inner-city and poring over real estate ads. We looked at thirty different buildings over the next year but nothing seemed quite right. While our search for a building continued, we partnered with Palm Beach Atlantic University and the Gathering of Men in 2001 to start Impact Basketball Camp, where we offered four days of basketball training and mentoring to young men in the community. More than 90 boys signed up for the camp.

I was grateful for our newfound partnerships with Palm Beach Atlantic University and the Gathering of Men, but yearned to increase our volunteer pool even more. I quickly learned, however, that recruiting volunteers to work in the inner-city was no easy task. We had been in contact with local urban churches but many of them seemed at a loss as to what they should do. The youth we worked with were often troubled, so the churches were usually hesitant to include them in their activities.

Likewise, many suburban churches were just as hesitant to get involved in the inner-city, fearful of entering what they perceived to be a dangerous environment. I understood their hesitation, but I reminded them that Scripture commands us to care for the poor regardless of whether it is "safe" to do so or not. As Christians, we were called to minister to "the least of these" that Jesus talked about in Matthew 25. God promises to be with us and give us the wisdom we need.

Help Arrives

As we continued to pray for more volunteers, a young man drove up to our office in a Jeep one day and told me that he wanted to work with inner-city youth. I was excited but also skeptical, wondering how long this white guy from the suburbs would last. If the kids rejected him or he found himself in a dangerous situation, would he stay? He became a volunteer and what a blessing it was to see God use this young man by the name of Chris Tress. Chris and I shared empathy for the fatherless and poor children in the community, and he became a close friend and trusted ministry partner who is still with the ministry. You will hear much more about Chris later.

Kerry and I knew that we could never accomplish our vision alone and God has faithfully added to our team every year. There were times when I was hesitant, for I knew the sacrifice required to work in the urban community. Yet God did not hesitate and has called and continues to call many to make sacrifices for the poor. There are times when I cannot reward my team and donors the way I would like, but I am comforted by what Jesus said about His reward in Matthew 10:42: "And if anyone gives even a cup of cold water to one of these little ones because he is my disciple, I tell you the truth, he will certainly not lose his reward."

Perhaps as you read our story, you feel a stirring in your own heart toward the poor and destitute. Later in this book, I will give you some ideas of how you can be involved with UYI and the poor. But for now, just be open to what the Lord is saying and don't try to figure it out on your own. Just read on, and as you do, pray, "Lord, I submit to Your will, whatever Your will is." God will guide you as He has guided me and He will change your heart as He changed mine.

CHAPTER 6
MOVING INTO THE COMMUNITY

In 2001, Chris Tress came on staff and raised his own salary, the meager amount of $10,000. One of his main responsibilities was to run a weekly outreach for fifty kids at the Salvation Army Northwest Community Center on Rosemary Avenue in West Palm Beach. One evening when Chris and the kids were outside playing, a car stopped on the street in front of them and someone in the car began firing shots at an apartment complex across from the center. Thankfully, nobody was hurt and no one in the complex fired back at the car. If they had, Chris and the kids would have been directly in the line of fire. Chris has described this as one of his scariest encounters in the 'hood, but he pushed aside his fears and continued his work.

A few years later, he met his future wife, Colleen, through UYI and I had the privilege to marry them. Performing the ceremony for Chris and Colleen reminded me that I am not only a father to the kids in the community, but also a father to the staff who work with me. Chris served as UYI's director of ministry and pastor of

Bow Down, our hip-hop worship service. Chris, Colleen, and their children now live in the community, providing a stable family model to declare without words what we preach and believe. Chris is also my successor as President of UYI, a story which I will tell you later.

Rachel

One girl who I met through our weekly outreach at the Salvation Army was Rachel. She came to play ball, but didn't have any interest in Jesus. One night while Rachel was playing basketball in the gym, the whistle blew to indicate that the game time was over and the kids were to come together to hear the message. Rachel was so startled by the sound of the whistle that she accidentally fell down on the basketball court, hurting one of her knees. Our staff called me into the gym, and I picked her up off the floor and carried her to my car. I drove her to the hospital where doctors confirmed she had torn ligaments in her knee. While we were at the hospital, I met her mom and brother and her life story began to unfold.

Rachel was born in prison as a drug baby; her mother and father were addicted to crack cocaine. When she was two years-old, HRS came to her house and took Rachel and her three siblings away from her father who was a single parent addicted to drugs. Even though Rachel was only two, she remembers seeing the tears falling from her father's eyes as the HRS van pulled away. When Rachel was ten, she discovered that her mother had AIDS. She really didn't understand the disease, but could see that her mother was losing a lot of weight and was quite ill.

One night, Rachel's mother crawled into her bed

and tearfully asked her daughter to hold her because she was in so much pain. "All I could do was wrap my arms around my mom and whisper a silent prayer to God," Rachel said. She didn't know how else to comfort her ailing mother. Rachel was heartbroken when her mom finally passed away. She later told me the only thing that had kept her strong through that time was the UYI staff. She said, "I knew God had placed you all in my life so I would have somebody to help me cope with the storms that came."

Rachel gave her life to Christ at an Urban Youth Impact outreach event when she was thirteen. Soon after, Rachel's newfound faith was seriously tested. She learned that her closest friend and role model, her brother Jeremiah, had contracted HIV. When both her mother and brother passed away within days of each other, Rachel wanted to give up on life. She couldn't understand why God would allow something so awful to happen. She has since told me that when two people walked out of her life, more than fifty walked in. Rachel was referring to the staff and friends she had made through UYI. Her family at UYI stepped in to support, love, and encourage her through the hardest time in her young life. This is what I had always hoped we would be able to do and it was truly happening.

Rachel went on to graduate from high school in 2005. She is the first person in her family to have a high school diploma and also graduated from Palm Beach Atlantic University with the help of a scholarship provided by UYI. Rachel loves to rap and has recorded her own CDs. She has worked part-time at our office and at one point acquired legal custody of her three younger sisters. Rachel is a true survivor and a hero from the 'hood. I am constantly amazed that this young woman worked, went to school, and helped raise three children on her own. Rachel will give us an update on her life in the next section.

I am forever grateful that Rachel took an accidental fall in the gym one night. If she had not, it's likely that I would have never met her, heard her incredible life story, or been a part of the testimony she shares with people today. I know many other kids just like Rachel who are succeeding—or genuinely struggling to succeed. Is God calling you to reach out to the Rachel's in your circle of influence? Don't miss the opportunity for God to use you to make a difference in the life of a child.

A Ministry House

As our ministry continued to grow, God gave our staff the desire to move into the Tamarind Avenue community to represent the incarnate ministry that Jesus modeled by leaving heaven and coming to earth. We began looking for a house in the community, but most of the houses we saw were boarded up or being used as crack houses. In 2001, we found a house right off of Tamarind Avenue that was going to be auctioned. We began to pray that we could buy this house and turn it into a place where staff and interns could live, befriend their neighbors, and model the love of Christ in the community. We learned that the property would be auctioned for $13,000.

Over the next three weeks, we called friends and sent out letters asking for donations to help us buy the house. Just two days before the auction, we had raised only $5,000. We began to wonder whether God really wanted us to have that house. Then, the day before the auction, a donor pledged to give us $10,000. At that point, we began to wonder whether $15,000 would be enough. We anticipated a crowd of eager bidders at the auction, but we were the only ones to show up. Needless to say, the house was ours and we experienced God's faithfulness once again.

Many churches and businesspeople in the community rallied together to help us remodel the run-down property from a duplex into a three-bedroom, two-bathroom home that is now known as the Impact House. The Impact House is a vital part of UYI's ministry, where staff and interns live, are discipled, and reach out to their neighbors in the inner-city. Many young men have lived in the Impact House over the last seventeen years.

After-School Program and Leadership Academy

Many of the youth we knew were struggling to read and didn't have the support at home to improve, so we started an after-school program in 2001. We applied for and received a grant that allowed us to run the after-school program five days a week. The grant also allowed me to hire an educational director, Deb Hinson. Deb worked hard to establish the foundation of our after-school program, and we were able to tutor fifty kids every week. Receiving that first county grant was only the beginning of a long-term relationship between their funding and UYI. Since the after-school program began, more than eighty percent of the students in the program have improved their reading and disciplinary instances have decreased.

In the fall of 2008, Urban Youth Impact focused its

staff and programming to launch The Leadership Academy (TLA), an enhanced model of the after-school program for 115 students. In the past, the after-school program had consisted of tutoring, reading skills enhancement, and performing arts. Though these elements were essential to academic success, we had a vision to nurture the students in every area of life, including the spiritual.

The Leadership Academy goes beyond tutoring to equip the kids emotionally, physically, socially, and spiritually. Other programs that were previously separate from the after-school program have now been absorbed into the Academy's curriculum. In addition to academic enrichment, students are learning valuable leadership skills, working on community service projects, attending optional Bible studies, and being mentored by almost twenty full-time staff.

One of the concerns most often raised about urban ministry is the safety factor. People often ask me, "Aren't you ever scared?" There have been some tense moments, but I can honestly say that I have never been frightened for my life. I am more concerned for the lives of our youth and their families, lives that will end in tragedy or failure unless we, or others like us, offer a helping hand.

This is the beauty of knowing the Lord. I didn't loan my life to the Lord in 1983; I gave it to Him. I didn't entrust it to Him for safekeeping only to reclaim it when things got tough. From my perspective, I could lose my life in an automobile accident, yet I drive to the mall regularly. I could have a crane fall on my head walking downtown, but I still walk downtown. I live by faith that drivers will stay on their side of the road and cranes will stay where we park them. If I can have faith for those things, I can have faith to reach out and touch a lost world for the Lord.

What about you? What fear is keeping you from doing and becoming? What steps would you take today if you weren't afraid of what would happen to you or what people would say? I have found that urban residents are no different than suburban residents. They love their children, want a nice home, and want their children to read, write, and have a better life and future than they had. So what reason is there to fear? I am doing God's will, so I trust Him for all the outcomes. And speaking of outcomes, as we moved into the community, we were able to touch more and more people. In the next chapter, I want to tell you more of their stories and the partnerships we have established with like-minded people.

CHAPTER 7
MORE HELP FROM AND IN THE COMMUNITY

Not only did we find that we needed a bigger team to do the work God had called us to do, but we also had to partner and collaborate with other like-minded groups in our community. This was not always easy and we had to be careful to maintain our own values, standards, and beliefs while learning to work with experts in the field of education, social services, and counseling. I have prayed for God's guidance and He has given us many friends and partners who respect and appreciate our roots and calling.

Urban Youth Impact partnered with one such local organization called Hanley Hazelton that had years of experience working with dysfunctional families. One of our staff members was trained in their Roots & Wings parenting skills curriculum, which is based on thirty years of research that has identified factors placing children at risk for alcohol and drug abuse. Roots & Wings teaches parents how to influence their children in positive ways, especially when it comes to decisions about alcohol, nicotine, drugs, and other risky behaviors. The curriculum is designed for any parent but specialized groups include single, foster, and homeless parents as well as parents in recovery from chemical dependency.

Seventeen parents signed up for our first Roots & Wings class. At first, I was skeptical about how many of them would actually finish the class. Thankfully, the participants exceeded my expectations. At the end of the six weeks, only two parents had stopped attending the class! We held our first Parent Program graduation, a fabulous ceremony providing caps and gowns for the fifteen graduates. It was a joyful, emotional time and I saw many tears in the eyes of the parents. They were so proud of themselves for completing the course and bettering their families in the process.

Josh's Dad

Working with the parents, however, hasn't always given me warm feelings. I will never forget one encounter I had with a parent after I had to discipline his son. We had taken a group of boys to the Miami Dolphins training camp and met many of the players. One of the boys who came on the trip was Josh, and he was disrespectful during the whole outing and on the ride home. I decided that I was going to show Josh who was in charge by talking with his father when I brought him home. I knew his father was periodically at home but spent most of his time on the streets playing cards and drinking with his friends.

As I drove down Tamarind Avenue, I found Josh's father sitting with a group of men. Josh and I got out of the car and approached his father. I said, "Sir, I want you to know that your son has been extremely disrespectful to me today.

I won't put up with it anymore, so he is suspended from our program indefinitely." I expected Josh's father to be on my side but was in for a surprise. He looked at me and said, "Mr. Bill, I know you help our kids, but if you ever touch my son, I will go home, get my gun, shoot you in the head, and eat your brains. Don't ever touch him." Smelling the liquor on his breath, I knew it was best to just end our discussion and walk away. As you can imagine, I never had any desire to challenge Josh's dad again. Thankfully, he and I eventually developed an ongoing relationship based on mutual respect.

The Christmas Store

In the same year that we started our parent program, we also organized a special event called the Christmas Store. Since UYI's mission was to love, equip, and empower inner-city youth and their families to fulfill their God-given purpose, the Christmas Store was designed to empower parents and honor their role as providers. Rather than have an outsider bring toys to a family in need, the Christmas Store gave inner-city parents the opportunity to shop for free toys and then distribute the toys themselves.

The Christmas Store has since become an annual event and it is always a joyful time for the families. The event includes bike raffles, gift wrapping, food, and special giveaways just for parents. It's also a great opportunity for families who are not involved with UYI to become familiar with our services and to experience the love of Christ. The first year we organized the store, we ministered to 200 families by giving away 1,200 toys. Over the last twenty years, the Christmas Store has distributed 35,000 toys to more than 12,000 kids.

It is no accident that as God gave us more workers from the community that we were more effective in the community. There is always a danger that those who work with the poor can treat the poor like they are hopeless and helpless. We can come in to give them what we think they need instead of what they actually need. I have found that the poor can take care of themselves if we give them the resources and the support they need. Yet one of the resources we still needed so desperately was a facility that would enable us to do more and meet the holistic needs of our residents. This was our next test but God was—and always is—up to the test.

CHAPTER 8
THE DREAM COMES TO LIFE

As the months passed and our programs and outreach events continued to expand, my yearning to have a facility as a focal point for our activities only grew more intense. Some local leaders encouraged me to share my desire to build an outreach facility at a City of West Palm Beach commission meeting in 1999. I spoke to the commission about the need in the community and our commitment to build an outreach center. The City agreed to provide land for us, which started a four-year process of locating property where we could build. I was so excited that God had opened a door for us to partner with the City. We found a donor who committed two million dollars toward building expenses and we worked with a local politician who committed another one million dollars. My patience was greatly tested over the next four years, however, as planning, designing, and countless meetings prolonged the process.

After two years, we had a location and our designs were finalized and ready to go. At last, we were finally ready to draft a lease for the land at the amazing cost of $1 a year. During one of our final meetings with the City officials and the architect, a new man from the City wandered in and looked over our plans. "You can't build there," he announced. "There's a sixty-inch water main underneath that property, and if you want to move it, you'll have to pay for it." I was absolutely shocked. During four years of planning and discussions, had no other City official known about that water main? I knew we couldn't afford $200,000 to move one pipe so we could lease the land, so I walked out of the meeting completely deflated. Why did God allow us to plan that building for two years only for that door to close so unexpectedly? Memories of our days at the PARK Center flooded my mind and we were back to square one yet again. George Mueller once said, "The only way to learn strong faith is to endure great trials. I have learned my faith by standing firm amid severe testings."[11] This latest setback was a severe testing, indeed. God allowed this testing so I could examine my heart motive for the Dream Center. What was exposed was that it had become about establishing Bill's ministry and not God's purpose and glory.

Crossing Australian

Glenn Pate, our architect, urged me to check out a building that was across the street from our office on North Australian Avenue. I drove by it every morning as I came to work, but never thought much about it, even though it had been on the market for some time. I reluctantly agreed to arrange a walk-through of the building with the architect and our board chairman. On the day we visited the building, I became hopeful that maybe, just maybe, this building could become our outreach facility. It was 32,000 square feet and had the ideal space for an auditorium, classrooms, computer lab, and administrative offices.

The only catch was that the whole building needed to be gutted and remodeled for our needs. We made an offer on the property in 2003, starting a two-year process. Amazingly enough, the price never went up even though the market had grown and the property was appreciating in value. Also, we were the only interested buyers. Nobody seriously looked at the building during those two years. My excitement grew at the thought of finally being able to use that previously committed three million dollars to remodel the building.

In my excitement, I called the local politician who had committed the one million dollars and told her that we were within reach of securing a new property. To my surprise, she called back a week later and backed out. I was thankful that the other donor who had committed the two million dollars was still on board. Our negotiations with the seller were going well, so I contacted our remaining donor to tell him about the good news. Within a few months, he had to back out due to personal reasons. We were in the process of buying a 32,000 square foot facility and suddenly had no money with which to buy it.

In the midst of my disappointment and confusion, I kept reminding myself of Hebrews 6:12b: "Imitate those who through faith and patience inherit what has been promised." As I reflected on the four-year deal with the City that never came to be, I began to feel grateful that God had spared us from leasing land and building our facility on City property. Doing so would have complicated a lot of things. Now we had the opportunity to own a building with the final say on how we used it.

Moreover, I sensed that this building was supposed to be ours. Glenn, his wife Pat, Chris, and I began to take regular prayer walks around the property to anoint the building with oil. We prayed, "Lord, if this is where You want us, we believe that You will provide and make a way." During this season of waiting and prayer, when I secretly wondered whether the Dream Center was an unattainable fantasy, God provided special angels to encourage me to keep trusting. Those angels were Gary, Jan, Carl, and Marcia, who blessed me with timely encouragement, practical advice, and financial support. Their sacrificial giving helped keep the dream alive and I will always be grateful for their friendship and faith in my vision for an outreach facility.

Finally, on July 23, 2005, we purchased our soon-to-be Dream Center. What a day of celebration and praise to God for His faithfulness! I jokingly refer to our moving day as the day we "crossed the Jordan." In reality, we only crossed Australian Avenue. We started on the east side of Australian, where we had been working out of a 3,600 square-foot office with a monthly rent of $3,500. On the west side of Australian was our new 32,000 square-foot facility with a monthly payment of $3,400. We finally owned our own building and could use it however God wanted. Through faith and patience, God had provided in His way, in His time, and for His glory.

We began saving for renovations to transform the vacant dental manufacturing facility into the Dream

Center that we wanted it to be. Once we had raised enough money, we began to remodel the 32,000 square-foot building in phases. Phase I of the renovations readied 6,000 square feet for administrative offices and meeting rooms. God provided the $175,000 we needed to remodel and furnish this entire space. We moved into our administrative building in September 2005 and quickly settled in.

Back2School Blast

The following summer, the local church where I accepted Christ approached us with an exciting opportunity. They wanted to partner with us to host their annual Back2School Blast. After five years of hosting the event and surveying the families that attended, the church determined that more than eighty percent of the families lived in West Palm Beach and Riviera Beach, a far drive from the church's North Palm Beach campus. In an attempt to better serve the people in need, the church offered to take a primary role in planning the event if we would agree to hold the event on our property. I felt this was a strategic partnership that aligned well with Urban Youth Impact's mission.

The sixth annual Back2School Blast held at UYI's Dream Center was a success. We provided free backpacks, school supplies, haircuts, health screenings, and immunizations to hundreds of children. Maranatha contacted us shortly after the event to ask us if we would take over the primary responsibility of planning it. I was excited to have the opportunity to continue serving our families in such a crucial way, so we agreed. The seventh annual

Back2School Blast was also a success. We expanded the event with the help of new partnerships including one with the City of West Palm Beach. That year we gave away more than 3,000 backpacks.

As of this writing, the program no longer exists, having been replaced with other initiatives, but it played an important role in our development and ability to impact the lives of young people in our community.

Back to The Dream Center

Meanwhile, we were praying and saving to begin Phase II of renovations in the Dream Center. Before we could start renovating, we had to get a building permit from the City of West Palm Beach. This process took fifty-four weeks! It wasn't much fun to wait but we persevered. Phase II was a much more expensive undertaking than Phase I and took us three years to complete.

Phase II includes a two-story 12,000 square-foot education and medical building. The education building includes four classrooms, a spacious recreation area called the Chill Zone, a computer lab, and state-of-the-art equipment for 115 students. Though we had intended to use both floors for the education center, we partnered with First Baptist Church of West Palm Beach to house the Community Health Center, the church's free clinic, on the second floor. That clinic moved out of our building when Phase III of our renovations began in 2014 so we could utilize the space for our core mission to the community youth.

On April 5, 2008, we opened Phase II of the Urban Youth Impact Dream Center. The renovations cost $1.6

million and seeing the beautiful new facility was worth every penny! More than 200 guests attended our open house to tour the new building. Everyone gave thanks to God for the tool He had given UYI to touch our community. By God's grace, we were able to pay off our mortgage in 2015.

Impact Coffee Company

As I mentioned earlier, another dream of mine was to start a business to coincide with the ministry of Urban Youth Impact. The business would provide jobs for inner-city youth and additional funding for UYI. In 2008, Robert Craven, a local businessman, offered to help UYI begin a coffee business which we named Impact Coffee Company. As my staff and friends well know, I enjoy a steaming cup of coffee every afternoon so I was eager to jump on this opportunity.

We launched Impact Coffee Company in October 2008 and hired 18-year-old Samara to serve as general manager. We have also hired a few additional high school students to play an active role in every aspect of the business including manufacturing, distribution, and marketing. As the business grows, we will involve more students from The Leadership Academy so they can acquire the job and leadership skills they will need after they graduate from high school. Eventually, we concluded that maintaining this company required too many resources that we could not provide, and we closed the business in 2013, but I still have a love affair going with coffee.

My Family

Working among the urban poor is not a part-time

pursuit. It requires tremendous energy, stamina, and spiritual determination—along with a large dose of God's grace—to deal with the challenges, disappointments, and community expectations. On top of that, UYI has a young staff, all of whom are learning how to manage ministry, relationships, marriage, and young children on a tight budget. I have found that at times I must be a pastor, father, mentor, coach, cheerleader, arbiter, and creative leader. There are days when I have gone home exhausted and depleted of energy.

In the early days of the ministry, Kerry and I worked long and hard side-by-side. We found it difficult (or should I write that I found it difficult) to stop thinking about ministry when we got home. We would often talk about someone's problem or an idea for a new program or outreach. While that was a good thing, we eventually found that those discussions began to dominate our personal lives.

Along the way, Kerry took a smaller role in the day-to-day operations of UYI. It wasn't that she had lost her love or passion for ministry to the poor. It was just too much for both of us to deal with. As my leadership role and duties increased, Kerry began to serve as a consultant when the ministry needed her expertise. As our staff grew, along with the administrative complexities of grants, buildings, and human resources issues, Kerry found herself doing less and less.

As Urban Youth Impact grew, we encountered a painful paradox almost daily. While we were ministering to so many other children, we didn't have any children of our own. After twenty years of serving the fatherless kids and families in the 'hood, Kerry and I had finally accepted the painful fact that we would never have children of our own. The kids we ministered to were ours, so we celebrated with them and cried with them. Then in 2004, we were approached to adopt a baby girl named Rachel. I wondered, *Could she be God's answer to our prayers?*

We had no money to pay for the adoption but after much prayer, we said yes. The day after we committed to adopt Rachel, a close friend said he would help us raise the money we needed. Kerry's focus immediately changed from assisting me with the ministry to getting Rachel's room ready—and all the other fun things that mommies dream about doing when a baby is on its way.

Rachel Nicole Hobbs was born on August 18, 2004 in Cape Coral, Florida, just three days after Hurricane Charley devastated that area. We took her home two days after she was born. Within the next two weeks, Hurricanes Frances and Jeanne hit West Palm Beach and we faced the exciting challenge of caring for a newborn without any power in our house!

As I reflected on what God was doing in our lives by bringing Rachel to us, my purpose in life hit home like never before. I was really going to be a father to a fatherless child for the rest of my life! What a privilege and honor it has been for Kerry and me to raise Rachel in the ways of our Lord and depend on Jesus to guide us every step of the way.

These last fifteen years with Rachel have taught me so much, and I hope that fathering her has made me a better husband and minister to the poor. I have had to learn more about my Father's love so I could be a better father. I have been able to relate more effectively to parents now that I am one myself. And I have watched my wife become one of the greatest moms in the world.

In 2017, my staff and friends held a twentieth anniversary ministry party for my family. We were honored, humbled, and blessed as many friends and family gathered to celebrate the goodness of God in the midst of our work in the urban community. I heard from many of those present and it reminded me that God has been good to us, better than we deserve. I didn't realize that my longest "drive" would never be on the fairway but instead on the road to achieve my purpose to love, equip, and empower the youth and those called to minister to them in the inner-city. It's been a great ride, but it's had a few bumps and breakdowns along the way.

I never imagined that we would be able to do so much so quickly. God has always shown Himself strong — not because of who I am but because of who He is. I believe that we have done so much because we have a cause that is close to God's heart, the poor. We have made ourselves available and He has done the rest. In the process, we have been changed as we have worked with the poor and perhaps received more than we have given. Ephesians 3:20 has become our reality: "Now to Him who is able to carry out His purpose and do superabundantly more than all that we dare ask or think infinitely beyond our greatest prayers, hopes or dreams, according to His power that is at work within us" (AMP).

As I mentioned in the last chapter, we must always guard against a "do gooder" mentality as though we are doing the poor a favor when we help them. I am in no way superior to anyone with whom or to whom I minister and

I can only maintain this attitude when I am careful to understand and apply the principle of servant leadership, which we will discuss in the next chapter.

CHAPTER 9
SERVANT LEADERSHIP

Jesus gave the best explanation for the concept of servant leadership in Mark 10:42-45:

> Jesus called them together and said, 'You know that those who are regarded as rulers of the Gentiles lord it over them, and their high officials exercise authority over them. Not so with you. Instead, whoever wants to become great among you must be your servant, and whoever wants to be first must be a slave of all. For even the Son of Man did not come to be served, but to serve, and to give his life as a ransom for many.'

We who are at UYI are called to serve the poor in our community, but we have encountered many problems and setbacks along the way. Sometimes the work is discouraging and painful, especially when a young person for whom we have so much hope is overcome by temptation and stumbles. In the urban community, the temptations can lead to drug addictions, teen pregnancy, or crime. We must always remind ourselves that we are doing God's work, that He is in control, and that we are planting seeds that will take years to overcome the suffering, sin, and pain in the inner-city.

We cannot be content, however, to simply meet the needs caused by ongoing problems and dysfunction. At some point, we must deal with root causes. We must not only serve our community but also lead our community. We must not only fight unemployment, but also provide jobs. We must not just feed residents, but we must also teach the residents how to feed themselves—which may mean confronting systemic racism that hinders our residents from feeding themselves. There are times when we must educate our suburban politicians and brothers and sisters sitting in the pews as to what the real issues and needs are in the community. We must expose them to what the poor experience every day and then call the Church and the community to be part of the solution and not part of the problem.

I have found that maintaining an attitude of servant leadership is essential if we as urban workers are to maintain our balance and not become burned out, frustrated, cynical, or bitter. After twenty-two years of ministry in the urban community, please allow me to get a bit philosophical for a moment and explain what servant leadership entails.

Someone once defined servant leadership as meeting the highest priority needs of another person. Someone else described it as giving some of the power of leadership to others—to empower them to be all they can be. Leaders have power but power can corrupt if it is not used for the benefit of others, as Jesus warned in Mark 10.

The Bible has a lot to say about being a servant

and I could quote many passages from the Old and New Testament to illustrate this point. In the Old Testament, the word *ebed* is the Hebrew word for servant. Many of the Old Testament characters are called the *ebed* or servant of the Lord. This means they were at the complete disposal of the Lord and also at the disposal of the people He called them to serve. I made myself available to the Lord as His servant, and He in turn made me a servant of the poor.

There were some servants who worked for their masters for pay (see Deuteronomy 15:12-15). There were times when I had to trust the Lord, my Master, for my own provision while I was working to secure provision for others. I have served and led the people while I have also served God, and God has always been faithful to provide.

There were also some servants who had given up all personal rights in order to serve their masters. The Bible calls this type of servant a personal bond slave (see Deuteronomy 15:16-18). To be a servant leader, I had to relinquish all of my personal rights in order to serve my Master and to serve those he has called me to serve. This was often humbling and at times awkward, but I am growing in my concept of who I am in Christ.

Let me give you an example. There are times when a youth or a parent comes to me for help. I look at their situation and am tempted to make all kinds of judgments or recommendations. I want to say, "How could you have made that decision? What were you thinking?" I must remember, however, that I am a servant leader and so I must serve and lead. Therefore, I take steps to serve their practical needs even as I position myself as a leader to teach and train them to make better life decisions in the future.

Being a servant leader does not mean I am soft or blind, although some would interpret it that way. I have had to stop serving people whom I loved because they only wanted me to be a servant and not a leader. I have had to remove some staff from my team because they only wanted to lead and not serve. If anyone is going to be effective in the Lord's great urban mission fields, we are going to have to learn what servant leadership means.

Please don't misunderstand me. It is a great privilege to do what I do and servant leadership isn't just for urban workers. It's for *all* of God's workers whether they are called to work with down-and-outers or up-and-outers. In my last twenty years of urban ministry, it has required sacrifices as an individual and a family. This is why our motives and values must be appropriate, for they will most certainly be tested in ministry.

Along with an attitude of servant leadership, I would suggest three values that are vital to keep in mind if we are to persevere in this work. They are:

1. *A willing heart*—Jesus said that His life was not taken from Him, but given freely (see John 10:18). Likewise, Stephen, the first Christian martyr, offered up his life voluntarily (see Acts 7:59-60). You may not be asked to die for your faith, but Jesus does expect you to die daily to your self-interests so you can serve others (see Luke 9:23). This must be done willingly and not grudgingly for that will lead to attitude problems in the long run.

2. *A life of sacrifice*—King David said he would offer no sacrifice to God that cost him nothing (see 2 Samuel 24:24). Serving God can be costly and the cost is more than just financial. You may be asked to give up your dreams, your expectations, your reputation, or your retirement fund. You must be willing to give to God whatever He asks in order to enrich others.

3. *A consistency of purpose*—You are to pour yourself "out for each other in acts of love," doing for others what they cannot do for themselves. You are to do this consistently, and not in "fits and starts" (Ephesians 4:2, *The Message*). Many people remember the poor at Christmas, but God wants us to remember them all year long.

When Rickie and Rachel came into my life, I was called to serve them like I would serve Jesus. It didn't matter that they were younger than I, or poorer, or of a different race. It didn't matter what mistakes they or their parents had made. When they came to UYI, my job was to serve them and lead them to a better life so they could carry out God's will for their lives. I did not and could not determine what that will was. I didn't get a vote and God did not consult me. He assigned them a purpose. He then required me to help them accomplish that purpose.

That meant that all my gifts, experience, and resources were at their disposal. Whether they said thank you or not, expressed appreciation or not, turned out the way I wanted them to or not, it was still my role to be a servant leader. That also meant that when I encountered racism or insensitivity in the community or in the Church, I had to speak up lovingly but firmly. I could not condemn but I could not shrink back. That is also part of being a servant leader.

When I saw someone whom God had blessed with many natural blessings, I had to urge and exhort them to share some of those blessings with the poor. I could not manipulate them into doing so for a servant leader always influences and never coerces. All of these roles were required of me as UYI's founder and president.

Servant leadership is the reason we chose to buy a house, renovate it, and have UYI team members live among the poor. It is the reason we have taken salary reductions in lean times and trusted God even in times of abundance for our own provision and support. It is why we weep with those who have lost loved ones to drug overdoses or gang violence and why we attend funerals as well as graduations for our UYI youth.

What is God saying to you about being a servant leader? Jesus is our model and we must always strive to represent Him accurately. I want to continue to offer my gifts, talents, and time to urban residents as God gives me strength, and I want to enlist as many fellow servant leaders as possible in the cause of urban missions. In the next chapter, I will tell you how you can join me in this important work. I hope you will read this not only for its content, but also to help you understand and clarify your own role in the huge task of reconciling and redeeming the lost for Christ.

CHAPTER 10
"BECAUSE I SAID SO"

If you have been blessed with children of your own, you know they go through the stage of asking, "Why Daddy? Why Mommy, why, why, why?" Though I loved my little girl when she came of age to ask, I would be lying if I said it didn't frustrate me at times when she did that.

I can't help but wonder if we, as God's children, sometimes do the same thing to our Heavenly Father. How many times do we ask the same questions again and again? And how many times do we ask the same questions just to avoid taking action? I don't know if anything frustrates our loving and all-knowing Father, but I'm sure He could easily respond in the same way. When we ask, "Why should we help the poor?" He lovingly says, "Because I love them and said to do so. Just look at my Word and see what I've said."

God repeatedly directs us in His Word to help the poor. Look at Jesus' heart when He saw the crowds of hurting and needy people as expressed by four different translations of the same verses:

- When he saw the crowds he had compassion on them, because they were harassed and helpless, like sheep without a shepherd. Then he said to his disciples, "The harvest is plentiful but the workers are few. Ask the Lord of the harvest, therefore, to send out workers into his harvest field'" (Matthew 9:36-38).

- When he saw the throngs, he was moved with pity and sympathy for them, because they were bewildered (harassed and distressed and dejected and helpless), like sheep without a shepherd. Then he said to his disciples, "The harvest is indeed plentiful but the laborers are few. So pray to the Lord of the harvest to force out and thrust laborers into his harvest" (Matthew 9:36-38 AMP).

- When he looked out over the crowds, his heart broke. So confused and aimless they were, like sheep without a shepherd. "What a huge harvest!' he said to his disciples. "How few workers! On your knees and pray for harvest hands!" (Matthew 9:36-38, *The Message*).

- He felt great pity for the crowds that came, because their problems were so great and they didn't know where to go for help. They were like sheep without a shepherd. He said to his disciples, "The harvest is so great, but the workers are so few. So pray to the Lord who is in charge of the harvest; ask him to send out more workers for his fields" (Matthew 9:36-38 NLT).

The ethic of generosity toward the poor is best expressed in the person and work of Christ according to 2 Corinthians 8:9: "For you know the grace of our Lord Jesus Christ, that though he was rich, yet for your sake he became poor, that you through his poverty might become rich." Christ's example should help us see our responsibility to use some of the wealth God has entrusted to us to glorify Him by sharing with the poor. The Apostle John made the following statement concerning our need to help the poor:

> We know love by this, that He laid down His life for us; and we ought to lay down our lives for the brethren. But whoever has the world's goods, and sees his brother in need and closes his heart against him, how does the love of God abide in him? Little children, let us not love with word or with tongue, but in deed and truth (1 John 3:16-19 NAS).

Christ's love should move us to compassion for those who are suffering in poverty. Jesus clearly taught about caring for the poor when He described this scene at the last judgment:

> "Then the King will say to those on his right, 'Come, you who are blessed of My Father, inherit the kingdom prepaid for you from the foundation of the world. For I was hungry, and you gave Me something to eat; I was thirsty, and you gave Me something to drink; I was a stranger, and you invited Me in; naked, and you

clothed Me; I was sick, and you visited Me; I was in prison, and you came to Me.' Then the righteous will answer Him, saying, 'Lord when did we see You hungry, and feed You, or thirsty, and give You something to drink? And when did we see You a stranger, and invite You in, or naked, and clothe You? When did we see You sick, or in prison, and come to You?' The King will answer and say to them, 'Truly I say to you, to the extent that you did it to one of these brothers of Mine, even the least of them, you did it to Me'" (Matthew 25:34-40 NAS).

The book of Proverbs also has some striking promises and warnings in the area of caring for the poor:

- "He who oppresses the poor taunts his Maker, but he who is gracious to the needy honors Him" (Proverbs 14:31 NAS).

- "One who is gracious to a poor man lends to the Lord, and He will repay him for his good deed" (Proverbs 19:17 NAS).

- "He who shuts his ear to the cry of the poor will also cry himself and not be answered." (Proverbs 21:13 NAS)

- "He who gives to the poor will never want, but he who shuts his eyes will have many curses" (Proverbs 28:27 NAS).

- "The righteous is concerned for the rights of the poor; the wicked does not understand such concern" (Proverbs 29:7 NAS).

Author and Compassion International president, Dr. Wes Stafford, perhaps wrote it best:

> Poverty is a large complex of issues, and Jesus spoke to every one of them. Our response must not be simplistic. It must cover as much ground as He covered. It is at this point that someone is sure to protest, 'Well, didn't Jesus also say something about 'the poor you have with you always?' This problem has been with us for centuries, and it's never really going away.' Don't stop in the middle of Jesus' sentence! His point was not that poverty is chronic in our world so don't worry about it. What He actually said that day in the temple was, 'The poor you will always have with you, and you can help them any time you want. But you will not always have me' (Mark 14:7). We do not have the option of ignoring poverty. We are called to be Christ's hands, Christ's feet and Christ's voice. Even a simple cup of cold water given in His name, He said, is like a gift given directly to Him. Who would skip that opportunity?[12]

I join Dr. Stafford in saying that ignoring poverty is not an option. Our only option is to respond and cover as much ground as Jesus covered. I encourage you to take the time to get alone with God and ask Him how you can and should respond. Don't be afraid of what God might say; rather, be afraid of not seeking His wisdom. Don't worry about feeling overwhelmed by the size of the task. As Mother Teresa said, "We cannot all do great things but we can each do small things with great love." He has given you gifts and resources to use for His Kingdom and He will lovingly draw you into His perfect will.

I often find that when people believe they cannot do a lot they tend to do nothing at all. Because they cannot give a lot they may not even give a little. If God has spoken to you as you have read my story, then perhaps you should consider getting involved with UYI in a small or major way. The only important thing is that you do something in response to what God is doing in your life and heart. Here are some things for you to consider:

- Giving
- Praying
- Volunteering at our programs or special events
- Interning
- Joining our staff
- Financially supporting current staff
- Making church presentations
- Hosting fundraisers
- Funding special projects
- Mentoring youth
- Joining our board of directors or advisory council

My staff and I would love to have you involved in this great project that we know is bigger than any of us because God is involved. We have wept, it's true, but we've also celebrated—and celebrated often. We've had our failures, but we've also enjoyed many more successes. And through our tears and our joy, we have confessed our own poverty so that we may better serve those who live in poverty every day. As Henri Nouwen wrote:

> When we are not afraid to confess our own poverty, we will be able to be with other people in theirs. The Christ who lives in our own poverty recognizes the Christ who lives in other people's. Just as we are inclined to ignore our own poverty, we are inclined to ignore others'. We prefer not to see people who are destitute, we do not like to look at people who are deformed or disabled, we avoid talking about people's pains and sorrows, we stay away from brokenness, helplessness, and neediness. By this avoidance we might lose touch with the people through whom God is manifested to us. But when have discovered our own poverty, we lose our fear of the poor and go to them to meet God.[13]

Pray, ask God, and then get in touch with us. Our contact information is at the end of this book, or you can go to our website at www.urbanyouthimpact.com. There are plenty of lives to touch, families to help, and also an abundance of service and ministry opportunities for you to embrace. Join with me in this great work of touching the lives of our urban poor with the love of God. I look forward to seeing you on the mission field with us.

SECTION TWO
2008 TO THE PRESENT

In this section, I want to share with you the things that have happened since my first edition was published in 2008. Along the way, we have learned a lot, sometimes from our mistakes, but we have also had a few more success stories that I want you to be familiar with.

CHAPTER 11
WHAT HAS HAPPENED SINCE 2008

Now it's time for me to tell you the rest of the story, as radio celebrity Paul Harvey used to say. My first book ended with the ministry in 2008 when we were just moving into our new facility. So much has happened since then, and that is why I wanted to revise this book to tell about the last decade of God's faithfulness. Let me start with Vision 20/20, which was established in 2012 to replicate what we have done at our main campus.

We identified seven pockets or concentrations of urban poor where youth are most at risk due to teenage pregnancy, single-parent challenges, crime, educational deficiencies, and addictions. Unless there is some kind of a change or intervention, the poverty cycle will continue. And so, now that we have established West Palm Beach, we've launched works in Riviera Beach, Boynton Beach (the other five areas are Lake Worth, Lantana, Delray Beach, Pahokee, and Westgate). As we have gained exposure, expertise, and credibility, churches have recognized their own responsibility to impact their cities. Rather than reinvent the wheel or relearn lessons we have, we have developed Kingdom partnerships with local churches to do the ministry and share resources and information.

Bow Down Church

I wrote about Chris Tress in the first version and section of this book, but let me reminisce once more about who Chris is and the price he paid to become the next UYI president. I remember when Chris pulled up in his Jeep, driving down from Jupiter to our small, 800-square-foot office, saying he wanted to volunteer. I was desperate for help, but I also realized that if people were going to volunteer and get involved in the lives of kids who were already broken and felt rejection, we didn't need some fly-by-night commitments that said after three months, "I've had enough." Therefore, I set the bar high for Chris, and he started coming to our outreach events on a regular basis.

He tells the story that one time he called me on the phone and said he couldn't come. I shot back, "What do you mean you can't come because you have car problems? You've made a commitment to the kids. You need to be here no matter what." I saw him respond by riding his bike ten miles to the outreach, which showed me his commitment level and faithfulness.

Those outreaches on Thursdays were a big deal. I discovered after we started that the youth and volunteers called that meeting Bill. They tried to name it, but they could only come up with Bill. One day, a young man came to know the Lord at one of the outreaches and I said, "Chris, take him home, meet his mom, and follow up." As Chris tells the story, he went home, but there was no mom. The house had children in it, but the refrigerator was empty, and they were all alone. Chris was blown away. All of a sudden, he saw the reality of the conditions in which many of the kids were living. They looked good on the outside, maybe they played basketball well or said the right things, but then they went home to hell.

Chris says that was the turning point for him when God introduced him to the call to the fatherless and his need to lay down his life to care for these kids. About a year or so later, Chris decided to move into the inner city. I went to auction to bid on a crack house, and we were the only ones there who wanted it. We bought it for $13,000, remodeled it, and Chris moved into what we named the Impact House. He began the Incarnate Ministry with a couple of the staff. He lived his call by walking the streets, and I watched him grow to the man he is today.

Eventually, it was time for him to become director of ministry. We traveled to different locations to see how they did their inner-city ministry. Many of those ministries were conducted through church, and that similarity and pattern kept popping up. In my mind, I was thinking, *Oh no, we don't need another traditional church. There are 15 in the community already.* Chris had made such great sacrifices and everyone who met him could see there was something different about this young man.

So in 2011, I called Chris in and said I felt it was time to birth a church and felt God was calling him to do it. We would work together and partner, but I felt God was going to empower him to do what he was called to do. And I have seen Chris continue to learn, humble himself, and be strong. Our relationship has been exceptional. We are two strong leaders who bang heads every once in a while, but when we're done, we humble ourselves, pray, and keep moving forward. Chris is like a son to me and I am a proud spiritual father.

We saw the need to birth a church, but knew because of the special needs in the community that there had to be a partnership with UYI, our non-profit. UYI could provide practical training, but then the church could raise up disciples, and the two of us could work together. If the calling and anointing were not the same for both entities, we could have done like some other churches who went into the hood and said, "That's a nice idea. Here's a few cookies, and we'll see you later."

Chris and I agree that we will have partner churches in all seven areas we branch out to after this first one. The person who pastors a church must have the same calling as the non-profit to the inner city so they can work together. When we look at what's happening in West Palm Beach with our Dream Center, we have seen the church come alongside and UYI has empowered the church by allowing them to use the facility, save money, and use our vans. We have shared resources and partnered together, and it has become a phenomenal Kingdom relationship. The church is now reaching hundreds of kids a week in outreach that perfectly complements what we are doing in our other programs.

The Dream Center Progress

We had just opened phase two of our building, the Dream Center, when I finished the book in 2008. The renovation cost $1.6 million, but the beautiful new facility was worth every penny. In the first edition, I described the health clinic and legal aid service that were housed in the Center. We discontinued both of those programs. In 2012, we had a waiting list for youth to come into our after-school program, and we had to make a decision to continue the health clinic and take care of teeth and eyes, or keep our focus on our kids to love, equip, and empower them.

We reached an agreement that the medical clinic would move out of the second floor. They found another location and we remodeled the second floor to add five more classrooms, which allowed us to bring in another 60 or 70 kids by expanding to 12,000 square feet. Then we could handle up to 130 youth on both floors.

The next step in our continued growth was to expand outside of the Dream Center. A door opened for us to begin work in Riviera Beach at the Stonybrook Housing Project, which at the time had 200 units with 300 kids under the age of 18, and only two fathers present. That was an unfortunate breeding ground for poverty and other issues that stem from fatherlessness. We were given the opportunity to use the project's outreach center and began programs there three days a week, seeking to build relationships, conduct sports outreach, and bring some other churches to Stonybrook.

In 2015, we still had 14,000 square feet of unused space that needed renovation, using it mainly as a warehouse for our Christmas Store annual event. I felt strongly that it was time to remodel and use that space, so our Complete the Campus Campaign was launched in 2015 to raise money so we could remodel the remaining 14,000 square feet in three phases.

In July of 2017, we opened the doors to phase one, comprised of 5,000 square feet, and it is a beautiful facility. As I write in 2019, we are in phase two, working to renovate 5,000 square feet with seven more classrooms, which will serve 84 kids, along with a state-of-the-art teaching kitchen. One of the things that has really expanded is our SMART or Science Meets Art Program. Once phase two is completed with the classrooms and teaching kitchen, phase three will renovate about 4,000 square feet. We want to go much deeper with the Science Meets Art Program, especially with the music and communication aspects. We are going to build out a recording studio, video studio, online radio station, podcasts, dance studio, offices, and a prayer room. That hopefully will be launched in 2020.

Phase one was launched in 2015, which was our first multipurpose auditorium space, seating 200 people and equipped with video screens and a full audio system. This became a facility where our performing arts SMART Program could have classes and hold performances. We could also use it to feed the community and for holiday events.

In 2012, the strategic plan called Vision 2020 called for the building renovations to be done by 2020. In 2018, I saw that we were not going to get it done, but we had already named it, so we have stuck with the name because Vision 2020 still gives us clear vision. We like to think we have "20/20" vision with our plans to expand into seven other key areas that need who we are and what we do. I am not discouraged that the building is going to take a bit longer than we thought, for every day I walk the halls and rooms and see what we are doing and how we are using what God has given us.

Summer Programs

The summer is a critical time for inner-city youth. Because moms are working and schools are out, the kids are out and crime is up. Many times during the day, Johnny, age 13, is in charge of the four, five, and six-year-olds. The challenges increase, so we birthed Summer Jam. Summer Jam is a miniature abbreviated version of The Leadership Academy. It goes from nine in the morning to four in the afternoon, feeding those who attend twice a day. Our capacity is 100 kids and it's a combination of education and field trips.

Palm Beach Atlantic University did a research project on us in 2015 to determine why transformation occurred for some youth and not for others.* The kids were privately interviewed who experienced change, and we learned that all encountered something summarized in the acronym EUP—Experienced Unexpected Pathway.

For example, change came to a young boy's life from an *Experience*, like when he went over to a family's home weekly for dinner. Another life began to change when a youth went on a college tour and began to see another side of the world that wasn't the hood selling drugs. A third life was impacted when a youth learned to play a musical instrument. We now want to provide as many experiences as possible, for we don't know which one God

---

* You can read this report at https://drive.google.com/open?id=0B9qZbK1 YQ8VbMjIwOFQzTFVFTHc.

will use to touch and change the course of a young life, which leads us to the **U** in EUP.

The second part of that change acronym is *Unexpected*. It was an unexpected pathway they thought could never happen, like someone paying for their college or enrolling them in trade school. They experienced something they never thought possible or even conceivable.

The last piece was *Pathway*. They began to see a vision or a pathway, and we came alongside them to help them walk the path. Today, we use the analogy that an inner-city kid exists or lives in something similar to a snow globe, but the stuff that's floating around is not snow, it's junk—the drugs, the crime, poverty, and all the temptations that are in there. People say to them, "Well, come on out. Just do it," but there are many barriers.

From our experience, when our kids have an EUP experience, the snow globe is smashed, and we now want to destroy as many snow globes as possible so they can walk out and experience the unexpected pathway our staff or programs provide. It's really an exciting thing when we talk to our staff about destroying snow globes.

Four years ago at a staff retreat, everyone made their own snow globe. It painted a picture to help us keep the kid's world in perspective. When an inner-city kid is in their snow globe, he or she looks outside and says, "I want those Nikes. How am I going to do that? What if I do this? What if I do that?" They must experience an unexpected pathway outside the snow globes, and our role is to break the glass and help them escape. I have always wanted to have a globe in my hand, throw it on the ground, and destroy it to visually demonstrate that.

We still take 44 kids out of the inner-city for the summer to Kids Across America in Branson, Missouri. They are exposed to the gospel and other youth in a summer situation. It's a life-changing experience, and studies show that camping works for these young people—which is another EUP.

Over the course of our 23 years of service to the West Palm Beach community, we have encountered many needs among our kids and families. We have always been strategic and decisive about which needs to target, yet we alone cannot provide solutions for every struggle in our community. Therefore, we have partnered with other organizations that assist us in our mission to love, equip, and empower our students in various ways to supplement what we are doing.

A great example of this is our partnership with Vinceremos Therapeutic Riding Center. This organization is a place where our students experience mental, social, and emotional healing through interactions with horses. They provide therapeutic help for specific children whose needs go beyond our ability to address. Although spiritual growth is not one of their stated values, we have seen spiritual development in the students who have been able to attend the 90-minute group sessions there.

Luis (going into fourth grade) loves to learn. He memorizes Bible stories in a detailed way and has a depth of knowledge on many different topics, including animals. He loves interacting with the horses every week. Luis's family escaped as refugees from Egypt several years ago and he has been without a father for many years. Despite the trauma and hardship which Luis and his family have gone through, he has demonstrated resilience and fervor for life during our Summer Jam program, ever eager to learn and connect with God, people, and animals.

Janis (going into 2nd grade) is overcoming physical, emotional, and social obstacles. She is gaining confidence in her ability to lead and express her needs (a skill she is currently developing during this stage of life). Janis has some physical conditions that in the past have prevented her from being able to do this. With the constant support of her parents, team leader, and our staff who encourage her daily in developing these skills, Janis is showing much more confidence in all these areas.

Kevin (going into third grade) demonstrates a true heart knowledge of God's love and will for him. Kevin entered our program one year ago exhibiting some intense negative behaviors and inadequate coping skills. However, with the support of our staff and reinforcement at home by his dedicated mother, he has been able to gain a sense of pride by making positive choices.

Kevin now verbalizes his needs instead of using a survivalist approach to get them fulfilled. He is now able to recognize that consequences accompany the choices he makes and knows the spiritual reason behind "doing the right thing," which is what he wants to do.

SMART

When I refer to going deeper by establishing the satellite outreaches in other local communities, one of the key passages that was a cornerstone for our thinking is found in Psalm 82:2-4, which talks about justice, the fatherless, and delivering them out of the hand of the enemy:

> How long will you defend the unjust and show partiality to the wicked? Defend the weak and the fatherless; uphold the cause of the poor and the oppressed. Rescue the weak and the needy; deliver them from the hand of the wicked.

That describes the poverty solution in that someone needs to go in and do the rescuing. We go in, we love them, equip them, and empower them, something we began doing in 2003 when the acronym LEE came into focus.

Part of our strategic plan was to *grow up* to the second floor; to *go deep* with the SMART Program; and then to *complete* and *repeat*. When the clinic moved out, we grew up. Then we went *deep* with SMART—Science Meets Art. We went deeper with the programming and deeper with the reading, doing pretests and post-tests for all students at the beginning and end of every school year. We went deeper in terms of staff involvement with kids. Go deep was a programming initiative through SMART that became more sophisticated. There are now more than 20 different SMART offerings. Our after-school program has Lego engineering, robotics, theater, dance, violin, piano, and on and on, made accessible to all students for a nominal fee. That's what I call going deep.

TLA—After-School Program

The Leadership Academy is the new name for our after-school program. As we moved into the education center and then grew up to the second floor, we had 12,000 square feet, handling 130 kids. When we moved in, the Lord put it on my heart to do a Dream Pledge. We were in the Dream Center, but the whole idea of a Dream

Pledge was taking the word *dream* and communicating key principles and ideas that we really wanted to speak and build into the lives of our kids.

- The D stands for dream big. We wanted to let the youth know they can dream big because Jeremiah 29:11 is true: "For I know the plans I have for you," declares the Lord, "plans to prosper you and not to harm you, plans to give you hope and a future."
- The R stands for respect and honor for family and authority.
- The E is to encourage others. We all long for positive words to build us up and not tear us down. Ephesians says we should not let any unwholesome word come out of your mouth, only that which gives grace to the hearer (see Ephesians 4:29).
- The A stands for always listening and obeying, and when we don't listen and obey, the youth learn there are consequences to their choices.
- And finally, the M stands for make good choices.

The Dream Pledge is communicated verbally each week and the team leaders use it as a teaching guide. *What does the Bible say about dreaming big? About respect and honor? About listening and obeying? About making good choices?* We use it to teach our core principles and values.

We supplemented the Dream Pledge with our

organizational values, which were developed in 2013 at a staff retreat with much input from everyone present. Here are the five values the staff developed:

1. *We Own Nothing.* Everything we have is from God and for God, including our lives; we have been bought with a price. We submit to the One we serve and abide in Him. From a place of gratefulness, we enjoy our role as stewards, doing more with less.

2. *We "Own" It.* As servants, we take personal responsibility for our role in everything. When we have a goal, we do everything we can to reach it. When we see that something needs to be done, we do it. When we fail or make a mistake, we own it. When we encounter problems, we find solutions. When we hurt others, we own it. When we are hurt, we forgive, even if not asked.

3. *We are Ambitious for the Mission and the Team.* In light of the crucial work before us, we sacrifice for the mission and the team. This is more than a job. Our work is on the heart of God. It is His work. It is bigger than us. It needs all of us, not an individual. We are committed. We are all in. We act in a way that is in the best interest of the team and the mission, not self.

4. *We Learn to Grow.* As individuals and as an organization, we will always need to get better. We look for ways to improve, and

when found, we will adapt and grow. We learn to get better and to be more fruitful and effective.

5. *We Give Our Best.* As stewards, doing things halfway is not an option. We are created in the image of an awesome, intentional, creative, and excellent God. This carries great responsibility. Where standards are clear, we do nothing less. Where standards are not clear, we do nothing less than our best.

In the past, I would have developed these values and passed them down, but these values were spelled out by the staff at a retreat. I think they are fantastic and will be much better kept and passed on because everyone had buy-in after they helped develop them.

As our programs and staff have increased, we have had to trust God for more money to operate the ministry. In the next chapter, I want to tell you about the fundraising we have learned to do in order to fund all the new things we have adopted. God has been faithful to provide, and we have tried to do things that are consistent with who we are and the mission we have. Let's move on to talk about that next.

CHAPTER 12
FUNDRAISING

There's no question Urban Youth Impact was built on big dreams and continues to dream big for each child and for the future of the community: "We know our God will do exceedingly, abundantly more than all we can ask, imagine, or even dream according to His power that is at work within us" (Ephesians 3:20 AMP). Below are the strategic initiatives that encapsulate the "dream big" vision in the early years.

1. Open a facility in the heart of the city.

    The Dream Center was opened in 2004 on Australian Avenue.

2. Train workers to serve the urban community.

    In partnership with Bow Down Church, Project 5:16 discipleship internship program was launched.

3. Launch satellite outreach centers to reach the largest at-risk populations in Palm Beach County.

    Stonybrook outreach site in Riviera Beach opened in 2012, weekly 10 volunteers and SMART program includes a dance class and DRUM instruction.

        Boynton Beach outreach site launched in 2014.

        Vision 2020 strategic initiative is to launch 5 more locations.

4. Establish a spiritual house in the city.

        Bow Down Church opened in 2011, led by Pastor Chris Tress.

5. Open a school program for tutoring and mentoring youth to enrich students academically, emotionally, and spiritually.

        The Leadership Academy was opened as an after-school program in 2008 and expanded with the SMART Program and Reframe Work Program.

Since I wrote the book ten years ago, it's been quite a journey. There were times when I sat back and reflected on our growth and God's goodness, and it brings me to tears. We have received some recognition and awards for our work but, of course, the main reward is to see the lives of the young people who have been touched and motivated by our LEE mission—to love, equip, and empower them for success.

In 2013, Urban Youth Impact was honored by the Bank of America with the Neighborhood Builder's Award, given to one group in Palm Beach County that made significant contributions toward making the County a better place to live and work. That award came with a $200,000 check.

In 2017, I was given the Impact Award by the Northwest Community Consortium, which is an organization established by grassroots church leaders. The

Northwest neighborhood is a historic area and is part of our ministry target zone. Every year they acknowledge leaders in the community who have had an impact. In 2017, I was honored to receive this award in recognition for our work to change the lives of inner-city youth. It was an honor to be recognized. It was quite significant for me to get that award after more than 20 years of working to birth a ministry in the urban community as a white guy, which was an uphill battle. It took many years to overcome questions, differences, and whatever other racial prejudices and stereotypes existed.

God strengthened me to be faithful, but it took people awhile to realize that Urban Youth Impact was real and wasn't in it for the short haul. We have been able to be faithful over a long period of time to serve, love, equip, and empower the youth in the community. When my peers and pastors, people who I respect and have grown up with in the community, recognized what I have done, it was encouraging. I know I have God's approval, but when men come alongside to acknowledge the work, it is really encouraging. It's helped me enter this season of my life and I am able to appreciate and celebrate it.

During the first eight years of ministry when I was with Youth for Christ, I abandoned my golf game. When I added a board member who owned a golf course, we reintroduced golf into my life in 2003 and hosted an annual tournament. It's been a great platform for us to reach out and bring in capable, successful people to hear about the ministry and play golf, and it has become a productive fundraiser. We always include a testimony of a young man from the community. One year we invited Paul Azinger, a

PGA Tour player, who shared at our tournament banquet. One of the interesting things about my transition from golf was I no longer served the rich but served the poor. Now God is using golf to help me be a bridge to connect both communities.

In the social setting of Palm Beach County, fundraising galas are quite popular. Now we also hold an annual gala dinner and invite prospective donors and current donors to be part of an evening where we celebrate our mission and hear testimonies from the kids. We obtain corporate sponsors and it's another way to bridge the gap between the haves and the have-nots, between the rich and the poor. There are people who are financially blessed but are somewhat stopped in their tracks whenever they realize what poverty exists in our community and the chance they have to make a difference. They learn that the youth are nice and are not there to steal their purse or be violent. The gala helps break down some social profiles that have been developed over the years.

The latest event that has reached a different section of the local population has been our 5K run called The Fall Stampede. We have a major commitment from Chick-Fil-A as a sponsor, so The Fall Stampede with the 5K run brings in the runners and the health enthusiasts. We had more than 750 runners in 2018 who ran the race down Flagler Boulevard, which is the main strip in West Palm Beach, and we raised close to $100,000 from that event. What's more, we exposed more people to the ministry and are looking for more opportunities to connect them to what we are doing.

No matter how big we get as a ministry, I foresee

that the mainstay of our organization's revenue will be individual donors. We have a growing mailing list, and many people contribute regularly to our special programs and to our operating fund. We often have people come through our Dream Center for a tour, and they are moved by what they see, often to the point where they give and keep on giving.

In addition, we have had many volunteers help us with our programs over the years. We have been blessed with incredibly talented and committed staff members who don't do what they do for the money, for the pay is not high. The work, however, is rewarding and many people have given the best of who they are to make UYI what it is today. They perhaps have been our greatest contributors and I am picturing many of them in my mind as I write this. I have stayed in touch with some, but others moved on to other work and ministry. I pray that the Lord blesses them for the difference they made while they were here, and I also bless our current staff, which is made up of some wonderful people who love the people whom they serve—and I think they are loved back.

Speaking of the people we serve, I promised in Section One to include some updates and stories from those who have been touched by our work. Some of these folks you already heard about in Section One, but others are new. What we do is not about the programs, the fund-raising, or the recognition; it's for the youth and the community, and I never get tired of hearing or reading the stories of how their lives were changed. Let's look at some of those stories in the next chapter.

CHAPTER 13
STORIES

I have provided many reports of people who were touched and transformed by Urban Youth Impact, but here are some stories of people in their own words, used with their permission and collected from personal interviews or taken from our twentieth-anniversary report.

KENDRIC: Second Chance for a Changed Life

I took a wrong turn early in life by holding up a convenience store for personal reasons and while in the commission of such crime I was shot multiple times and found myself serving a prison sentence. That could have been the end of my story, but I was given a second chance after reentering into society by Urban Youth Impact and a new beginning was formed!

Growing up in the Tamarind Avenue community at the time, there was very little positive influence which now that I am older, I wonder why that was.

While serving my prison sentence for attempted armed robbery, I had a lot of time to come up with a plan and realized I had a son to think about and had a desire to raise him to make better choices than I did. I knew UYI had a reputation of being a place of redemption, so I reconnected with my cousin, and he reconnected me with Mr. Bill.

Mr. Bill was gracious and hired me to do maintenance work around the Dream Center after giving me the task to detail his car with a $20 inside the cup holder — what a test. I was glad for a second chance in life and began to take full responsibility for my choices. I earned my GED, started raising my son, and got married. I was later promoted to Disciplinary Assistant at UYI Leadership Academy and loved who I was becoming.

Faith in Jesus transformed my life and priorities. I know there are more people like me, who would love the opportunity to leave the streets and start over. UYI is one of a few organizations in the Tamarind community pointing youth and adults in the right direction. I am the co-founder of Inner City Innovators Inc., whose mission is to inspire and empower inner city youth to embody the change they want to be in their community. I have been involved with Bow Down Church since 2009, and they are inside five communities nine times a week being either the hands or feet of Jesus loving on the people there.

I'm a Hope Dealer, on a mission to bring "Hope" which is why I started my company Pressure Cleaning Alliance to give others a second chance as it was done to me.

JEFFREY: First-Time Homeowner

My wife and I met Jeffrey when he was about five years old. We would pick up his brothers to go to our weekly sports outreach and he always wanted to come but was too young. When Jeffrey became of age, he met

Chris Tress who began to mentor him and introduced him to Christ. Even though he grew up in a dysfunctional home without a father, today Jeffrey is the very first home-owner in his family. He is a dedicated husband, father, and Christ follower in our local Tamarind avenue community. In addition, he has answered God's call and is on staff with Youth for Christ, reaching out and serving the kids in the community from which he came.

In Jeffrey's testimony of Urban Youth Impact, he shares the following that speaks deeply into what the work God, Chris, and Urban Youth Impact have done in him:

> "The biggest thing is that I want to be present. I want to be present with my boys. I want them to know who their dad is. I want them to know what their dad has come from, and that they don't have to come from that because our home is not dysfunctional. Our home is quite functional because we put Christ at the center of it."

Jeffrey and his wife have now welcomed another member to their incredible family through adoption. As we celebrate this wonderful event, we are reminded of the power of the adoption message; how we all are wanted and loved by God and can be adopted by Him into His family through His Son Jesus Christ.

RACHEL: A New Creation in the "Hood" From 13 to 30

I'm one of 18 kids, born while my mom was in prison. I was raped at age 6. My siblings and I were in and out of foster care. My mom and brother passed away from AIDS. I hated God and could not see any good in this life.

One day a friend invited me to Urban Youth Impact's sports outreach. I was 13 years old when God began to use Urban Youth Impact to turn my life around. *I put my faith in Jesus and found hope for a future!* I was the first person in my family to earn a high school diploma and attend college.

I wish I could say that I made all the right choices in my young adult years, but I dropped out of my last semester of college and gave in to the temptation on the street. My UYI friends did not give up on me and prayed for this prodigal to return home. When I finally realized the enemy of my soul wanted to destroy me and that God had a good plan for my life, I returned home.

I am proud to say that I graduated from college, I own a home, and I'm raising my three sisters. Who would have thought this wounded girl from the 'hood would experience the miracles of God as He continues to rescue my family and me.

I'm now in my 30s and grateful to Urban Youth Impact for loving, equipping, and empowering me. I currently serve on staff at UYI as a Team Leader in The Leadership Academy. I want to invest in the youth from the 'hood and show them that God has a plan for their lives even when circumstances seem hopeless.

REGGIE: The Fatherless Found a Father and a Purpose for Life

I grew up without a father and my mother was addicted to cocaine. My stepfather was physically abusive. At six years old, I ran away to live with my grandmother. At 15, my best friend Luke invited me to Urban Youth

Impact for football and Jesus. We spent our high school years playing ball and learning about God, but when Luke passed away our senior year of high school, I turned to the streets. I started hanging out with a bad group of friends and turned away from God.

Throughout the years on the streets I never forgot the words I heard about Christ during the Thursday nights I spent with Luke at Urban Youth Impact. One day, I thought maybe I was ready to get off the streets, so I went to visit Mr. Bill.

He knew I was running from God and not ready to surrender just yet. Soon after meeting with Mr. Bill, I was locked up in the county jail. And then less than a year later, I was locked up a second time. God finally got hold of me — He knocked again and this time I was ready. I made a decision to give my life to Christ.

Mr. Bill gave me a job at UYI doing facilities maintenance. Thanks to Bill Hobbs and the UYI family who loved me and empowered me to change my life. I've learned it's about accountability. We all walk in a world full of sin. It's an easy walk when you don't want to live to a higher standard. I see kids without fathers just like me and I want to help them find their God-given purpose. *It's my time to make sure a life is saved and changed.*

Alfons: A Walking Testimony

Alfons was a student at Urban Youth Impact who testified how UYI "has definitely impacted [his] life by loving, equipping, and empowering [him]." Recently, Alfons reflected on his time at Urban Youth Impact. He pointed out how quickly someone's life can be taken away, but also how quickly someone's life can be impacted. He mentioned there was a time when he would often receive phone calls about people he knew who were getting shot or hurt. He said he is thankful for his faith that carried him through those times, and he credits UYI for helping him maintain his faith throughout his childhood.

Alfons reminisced about UYI and how the bus would drive through the most at-risk neighborhoods, stopping at each house instead of just letting students off at the public corner "bus stops." It's interesting how our kids may not always express the gratitude for those small acts of everyday love, yet they truly do feel the love.

Alfons explained that he is a "walking testimony" as his life clearly shows. He attended and graduated from Florida Atlantic University with a BA in business administration with a concentration in entrepreneurship and played four years of outstanding football. He is now a business leader, man of God, public speaker, financial coach, mentor, athlete, and personal trainer. Alfons has now launched Brick by Brick Academy of Health & Wealth. We are very proud of Alfons and all our students. They are the fruit of Urban Youth Impact, and we are thankful to continue loving, equipping and empowering them to fulfill their God-given purpose.

ISAIAH: Dreams Come True for Those Who Believe

I was adopted by my grandmother at age six and moved to Florida in 2003. I grew up in Dunbar Village, right off of Tamarind Avenue. Despite the nightly gunshots I heard outside my window, I had big dreams and believed

God had something more for me than running with the street crowds.

UYI kept me out of trouble and helped me find my first job through the Summer Work Program in 2006. I'm thankful that Urban Youth Impact provided a safe place where I could do homework and play basketball.

When I was 14 years old, I adopted the UYI's mission to love, equip, and empower inner-city youth to fulfill their God-given purpose. I had a dream of becoming an attorney. My grandmother instilled a desire in me to make life fair for everyone. And I thought if I became an attorney, I could ensure justice, civil and human rights, social action and economic empowerment, childhood education, poverty alleviation, and environmental conservation.

In my sophomore year of high school, I enrolled in the Pre-Law Program at Palm Beach Lakes Community High School. UYI helped me with finding internships in law offices. I graduated with a B.A. in political science from Williams College. And I enrolled into law school.

In March 2016, I was honored when my longtime employer, Craig Goldenfarb, owner of the Law Office of Craig Goldenfarb, P.A. established a scholarship in my name. This scholarship will be awarded to high school seniors who are or were graduates of Urban Youth Impact.

I'm grateful to UYI for investing in me through my foundational years! They encouraged me to find my God-given purpose. As an attorney, I plan to "speak up for those who cannot speak for themselves; ensure justice for those being crushed. Yes, speak up for the poor and helpless, and see that they get justice" (Proverbs 31:8-9).

COLLEEN: One Little Decision Changed the Course of My Life

I did not grow up in the "hood" and was advised never to go on Tamarind Avenue due to its reputation for violence and crime. But my heart was moved when I heard there was a ministry called Urban Youth Impact reaching out to inner-city youth. I volunteered to drive a van to pick up girls and bring them to Bible study. Who would have thought this one little decision to volunteer would change the course of my life? I eventually joined the staff at UYI where I met Chris Tress. We fell in love, got married, and he moved us to the "hood." We've been here for more than 12 years, not exactly the dream a girl has for raising a family. God called us and we are blessed to minister together in the inner-city. I'm thankful that God gave me the grace to stick it out for so many years because I've watched many kids go through very hard times and work through to restoration.

In 2011, my husband and I started Bow Down Church to serve families with a disciple-making ministry in their community. We currently homeschool our two children and live in the inner-city with a vision to open more neighborhood church groups.

GRANDMA: A Story of Inspiration and Longtime Pillar of the Community

Grandma's story begins with her grandson, Thomas. He was a part of the Urban Youth Impact family since 1997 when Chris Tress mentored him. When Thomas' parents died, he moved in with his grandmother. His life inspired Grandma because she saw him thriving despite the odds of the community where more young men go to jail than to college. Grandma learned about faith in Jesus and completely surrendered her life to God. She was instrumental in the Family Empowerment Program and continues to be a pillar in the community. Her generous heart touches everyone she meets. And God continues to use her to bless others.

Little did she know, God had a big blessing in store for Grandma by providing a beautiful home for her and her grandkids. She had been living in a half torn down duplex with her three grandchildren. Colleen Tress was led to reach out to see if there was something to improve the living condition with a renovation, but God's plans were much bigger. Several people in the community and outside the community gave of their time, talents, and treasures to purchase a house to bless Grandma. She is now retired and still giving back to the community, has since gotten married, and is Grandma to many. Her favorite Bible passage is Psalm 23.

CHAPTER 14
UYI SUMMARY AND OVERVIEW

I have also mentioned many programs and special outreach ministries UYI started, some of which are still in operation, while others were replaced along the way. Here is a summary once again from our twentieth-anniversary publication to help you understand what we have done and are doing.

Year-Round Programs and Events

Through Urban Youth Impact's core programs, we serve nearly 230 youth every week with educational enrichment and job-readiness training while building lasting relationships.

The Leadership Academy

The Leadership Academy (TLA) is an after-school program serving inner-city youth in grades K-9. The primary goal is to prepare students during their formative years to succeed in life by providing academic assistance, character development, social skills, emotional guidance, and spiritual enrichment.

TLA serves up to 150 students daily during the school year through tutoring, computer-based literacy learning, faith-based instruction, life-skills and character-building lessons, mentoring, performing arts, field trips, and recreation.

SMART

The SMART (Science Meets Art) program offers extended learning opportunities for TLA students. There are over 30 specialized classes from computer graphics coding/software development to visual arts and music. Community partners, such as the Armory Art Center and Palm Beach Code School, teach and offer their expertise in the arts.

Reframe

The Reframe program started as a Summer Work Program. In 2012, UYI launched the year-round Reframe Work Program for in-school and out-of-school youth ages 16 to 22. Students have the opportunity to acquire life skills that are necessary for future employment. The program empowers young adults through mentorship, college prep, career exploration, as well as links to internships and jobs. Since the start of this program over 250 internship opportunities have been provided.

Summer Programs

Summer Jam

Since 2002, UYI offers affordable options for inner-city youth to attend the Summer Jam seven-week day camp held at the Dream Center in West Palm Beach. Activities include healthy cooking classes, art and photography, computer coding and design, outdoor sports, and field trips to the zoo, nature trails, water parks and more. The best part is the team building and God-Time devotion.

Kids Across America

Kids Across America is an overnight Christian leadership summer camp in Branson, MO. Since 2002, UYI has been loading up buses with 40-80 kids for a life-changing experience. Many inner-city youth have not had the privilege to travel outside of Florida, or even Palm Beach County and this camp provides challenging activities in an encouraging environment.

Annual Special Events

Back2School Blast

Although on a smaller scale than when it first began, the annual Back2School Blast equips students in the inner-city with backpacks full of school supplies and uniforms for the new school year. The event has expanded over the years to include health screenings, fellowship, and education for adults, along with a distribution of groceries to needy families.

Christmas Store

Since 2000, UYI has been bringing dignity to charity. The annual Christmas Store empowers parents of students in the UYI programs, along with the urban community. The event is held in December giving parents the opportunity to "shop" for free for gifts and toys to give their children on Christmas Day! Many local partners donate gifts for distribution. While the parents "shop," their kids have fun in the Christmas Village with many partners and volunteers.

Vision 2020

In 2012, Urban Youth Impact outlined an expansion initiative that enlarges the vision to serve the most at-risk children. Much has been accomplished and there's more work to be done by the year 2020.

- Grow up: We are growing up with our kids and have placed an emphasis on the older youth to provide a teen-friendly space, increased the Reframe Program, and launched the Entrepreneurial Academy.

- Go Deep: Enhanced the learning opportunities through The Leadership Academy with the SMART program offerings.

- Complete: Phase I is under way for the Complete the Campus project to build out the Dream Center. This includes a 250-seat auditorium for gatherings and chapel, a new lobby and portico, and audio-visual enhancements.

- Repeat: Launched two outreach sites in Boynton Beach and Riviera Beach.

Outreach Sites

Urban Youth Impact began in the Tamarind Avenue corridor and surrounding areas of West Palm Beach. Plans are underway to open five more outreach sites by the year 2020 in Delray Beach, Lake Worth, Lantana, Pahokee, and Westgate.

Children's Services Council (CSC) has identified the areas UYI serves as the areas with the most at-risk children based on numerous indicators such as poverty levels, school readiness, graduation rates, teen birth rates, and percent of children on free/reduced lunch among others.

Impacting Neighborhoods

Boynton Beach

The Boynton Beach UYI outreach site launched in 2014 and has been growing strong. With a strategic move from First Baptist Church of Boynton Beach to the Carolyn Sims Center, UYI is now able to reach even more kids because of the closer neighborhood proximity. Relationships are being built during the mid-week programming and every Saturday, middle and high school students gather for The Vibe.

> *"This year we encountered a kid that did not have college on his radar until taking a tour of FAU (Florida Atlantic University in Boca Raton) with Urban Youth Impact. He has since made a commitment to doing well in school so that he can attend college! The unexpected experience really motivated him to do well."*
> — Luther Menard, UYI Satellite Coordinator at Boynton Beach

Stonybrook in Riviera Beach

Urban Youth Impact began afternoon programs in 2012 with a pop-up program at the outdoor playground at the Stonybrook Apartment Complex in Riviera Beach. Soon after UYI obtained its own building which allowed UYI to serve the community at an even greater capacity. There are 10 consistent volunteers from Bow Down Church and PBA. Weekly programming includes: a girls' dance class and boys drumming, afternoon programs for kids 6-15 years old consisting of homework help, sports, crafts, games, spiritual enrichment small groups, and snack time. The outreach efforts have been expanded since opening because there are 200 families living in the apartments, including 400 kids, and there are only 3 fathers present. Those staggering numbers have stirred UYI to increase their outreach efforts.

> "It truly is an honor and a privilege to serve the community of Stonybrook. In a matter of almost two years we have gone from a once a week program to 4 times a week. Serving the students in the community with art, literacy and life skills. While having cooking classes for the parents and adults. My heart is full because I get to do this, it's not what we say but what we do. The Time is Always Now!" — Nestor Medina, UYI Satellite Coordinator, Riviera Beach

I hope you don't mind that I included in this chapter many things we had already discussed in earlier chapters. My reason to list them again was to make sure you caught the full scope of what we are doing, and where we are doing it. UYI has come a long way since 1997 when we started out with a dream and a heart to serve. We put up our sails, so to speak, and God blew into them to bring us to where we are today.

As grateful as we are for what we are doing, we are not satisfied, for we are aware every day that there are many more youth and communities that need a transformational touch from someone who not only cares but has the skill and experience to help them live a new life. We have more ideas and concepts we would like to develop, but we have to be patient and wait on God for His timing and provision. Let's talk about what it means to wait on God in the next chapter as we close out *Urban Impact: Love, Equip, Empower* in the next chapter.

CHAPTER 15
WAITING ON GOD AND SUCCESSION

One of the things God has been teaching me over the last three years is the concept of waiting. I am a guy with a lot of vision who is a recovering performance addict. When I first heard of waiting, I considered that we were wasting time and being irresponsible. Why would we want to wait when there is so much work to be done? My wife and I waited 20 years before we eventually adopted Rachel, and along the way had seasons where I thought, *That's really not fair, Lord. The word of God says children are a blessing of the Lord, so what am I doing wrong?* We waited and waited and waited, and then in the fullness of time, God brought Rachel forth. When He did, He got the glory. It was nothing that I created or manipulated. God has been teaching me that my hope and expectation come from Him (see Psalm 130:5 and Psalm 25:4 AMP).

That season continued as we had to wait to launch the final stages to finish the facility. We had a waiting list of children with needs and we were waiting on God. I kept thinking of "those who wait upon the Lord shall renew their strength" (Isaiah 40:31) and it dawned on me that those who wait are the ones who change. I realized that as I wait upon the Lord, I am changing because I am waiting in His presence. In the presence of God, it's not about me but rather about me decreasing. In His presence is where I take my thoughts captive to obey Him. It's about contemplative prayer as I focus on the Father and His love.

I also learned that waiting is receiving. Mary had to wait when the word of the Lord came to her through Gabriel. It didn't mean she wasn't actively seeking the Lord, but sometimes we have to wait on His timing. In addition to that, six years ago my wife had a physical attack, which we thought was appendicitis, but it was pancreatitis. The doctors took out her appendix and we thought everything was back to normal. Over the next six years, however, she had nine more pancreatitis attacks, and I couldn't do anything about it or fix it. I prayed, but I had to wait—and we are still waiting. I know God is aware of it and His hand is on it for good. God loves Kerry, but in the midst of those circumstances, we can get caught up in them and think that it is the final reality.

I am learning to "fix my eyes on Jesus, the author and finisher of our faith, who for the joy set before him, endured the cross" (Hebrews 12:2). I was waiting, but my eyes needed to be fixed on Him, not my wife, or my daughter, not the building or the funds. The Lord was and is using all that to draw me to Him and to break me so I will surrender to Him because He has my good in mind: "I am convinced and confident in this very thing, that He who has begun a good work in you will continue to perfect and complete it until the day of Jesus Christ" (Philippians 1:6 AMP).

Paul said he died daily (see 1 Corinthians 15:31). He also wrote that he had been crucified and it was no longer he who lived but Christ in him (see Galatians 2:20). The lesson in this season of waiting is a critical piece that I'd like to pass on to you. Waiting is not wastefulness. Waiting is difficult, but we must come to the end of ourselves, enter into His presence, be still, and know that He is God: "He says, 'Be still, and know that I am God; I will be exalted among the nations, I will be exalted in the earth'" (Psalm 46:10).

In another sense, the context of waiting is hoping. It's an active time when we exert ourselves to seek the Lord. Hebrews 11:1 says, "Faith is the assurance of things hoped for and the evidence of things not seen." Hope is the vehicle of our faith.

The Transition to Chris

My transition was spurred in 2015 when a major donor in our boardroom told me how thrilled she was with what we were doing. This woman is 85 and asked during our discussion, "This is so wonderful! What are they going to do when you are gone?" Her question stopped me in my tracks, and I began to ask myself a series of questions: *Is this my ministry or the Lord's? Am I a steward or a manager? What must I do to move forward in a transition and succession planning initiative?*

At first, the whole process was scary because, after all, in my mind UYI is my baby. Like with my daughter, however, who I will have to give away to a gentleman one day, the same is true for UYI. The challenge was to look in the mirror and ask myself how to be the best steward of this ministry as possible. My board and I began to study and look at how other organizations have transitioned. It was discouraging to find that a lot of the Christian organizations we looked at and talked with really have not been doing their succession planning well. Many of the ministry founders were strong and bullheaded and didn't want to let go.

One day I had the privilege to play golf with John Maxwell and I asked him what he thought the keys to a successful transition are. First, he said, leaders and especially founders usually stay too long. I asked who should make the decisions on timing and the right person to replace the leader, and he said from his experience, a third of the decision-making input should be from the founder, a third from the board, and a third from friends who will speak into the founder's life about it.

Therefore, I began that process by talking to the UYI board. I started meeting with two potential candidates who worked closely with me for many years, and then I went to the outside and sat down with three different mentors, told them the process and where we were at, and asked what they thought I needed to be working on. I introduced them to Chris Tress, the leading candidate, who had been with us for 20 years and is like a son to me. Chris had made great sacrifices for and shown great commitment to the ministry.

If you remember, earlier I had reported how Chris and Colleen moved into the community, bought a house, and brought their kids in, putting themselves at great risk. His first year he said he would live on whatever came in and in that first year, he earned $10,000. I had seen the commitment, sacrifice, calling, and anointing. It was obvious after two years of praying and talking that this was the man God had called to take over.

I was thrilled, but a little afraid because I had never done something like this before. I wanted to do it correctly and I knew I could be my own worst enemy by having unrealistic expectations about what should happen, when it should happen, and how well and smoothly it should happen. To counteract those tendencies, we sought wise counsel from people like my friend, Dr. John Stanko, and others who were strong leaders I loved, but who would speak the truth to me. The future of UYI and my legacy revolve to a great extent around how well we can answer the following questions. *Did he do it at the right time? Did he get out of the way? Did he empower the next person to do it differently and then serve as his coach and number one fan?*

In January of 2019, it was time and we invited our friends to an evening event that recognized the transition of the presidency from yours truly to Chris. I have been involved in many meetings in my lifetime, but I have never been in one like we had that January night. The atmosphere was charged with excitement, and friends from all over the county filled our auditorium in the Dream Center. Some of our board members spoke, I spoke, and then Chris spoke. We ended the evening as Chris and I desired, and that was the two of us on stage being prayed for by family, board members, and friends of the ministry. It was a grand time and I noticed afterwards that people lingered a long time, seemingly wanting to savor the moment.

Since then, I have stepped away from the day-today operations. I don't attend the executive team meeting any longer, unless I am needed. I am focused on advancing our vision through developing new strategic partnerships. It's been a new day but it is a great day, for I know the ministry is in good hands and I am free to do what I can still do to ensure the work continues.

Has it been a big adjustment for me? Yes, it has, but God is faithful, and I have a sense of peace and unspeakable joy to know that the work will continue after I am gone altogether, and the work we do is bigger and too important for one man's vision or energy to address.

As we close, let me speak from my new role in the development department and ask you to consider supporting UYI—if you don't already. Your investment in our work will ensure that we can write another section of this book. I probably won't be the one to write it, but someone else will tell you more stories about the new programs and the lives being transformed by the work UYI does. Your contribution will make it possible and the blessing that comes from giving to those who cannot give in return will be on you.

Thank you for reading and listening to my story, and I pray that the Lord's blessing will be on UYI as it has been since we began. And may He bless Chris and Colleen Tress, the board of directors, and all the staff, reminding them that our mission hasn't changed, for we are to LEE— Love, Equip, Empower inner-city youth to fulfill their God-given purpose.

EPILOGUE

Hello, this is Chris Tress. Bill has referred to me throughout this updated version of his Urban Impact story. Today, it is my honor to serve as the president of Urban Youth Impact. I took over from my father-in-the-faith, my mentor, my advisor, and friend, Bill Hobbs. I will always be grateful for Bill's role in my life and ministry. I am in the process of writing a book describing my experiences at Urban Youth Impact (UYI), so when Bill asked me to contribute to his book, I was happy to do so, for it got me in the flow and focus of writing what is on my heart. It is only proper that I should start my writing by summarizing for you what I know of Bill Hobbs now that you have finished reading the expanded story of his life in urban youth ministry. I am thankful for him and these past twenty years. When I think of Bill, I think of three things: boldness, faithfulness, and a caring heart.

When I think of Bill's boldness, I'll never forget one night when we were at camp around the time I began to volunteer at UYI. During the night, I was awakened by a man snoring. I was laying there and looked over at Bill, who was in a bunk bed like the rest of us. All of a sudden, Bill reached down, grabbed his shoe, and threw it at the guy! Everybody else in the room wanted to do the same thing, but Bill stepped up and did it. Some people need to get hit with a shoe to wake up, and Bill has done that for many people who were sound asleep, not recognizing the needs of the community around them.

I saw Bill's boldness on another occasion when

I was driving through our community. On the corner of Tamarind and Seventh, two people were holding signs saying "Try Our Jesus." Then I saw Bill Hobbs, sticking out like a sore thumb, as he blew a shofar. I did not grow up in a church, but that was not normal for most of the churches that I knew about. That's bold.

There's a verse that Bill prayed over me many times in Joshua 1:9: "Be bold and strong. Banish fear and doubt for the Lord your God will be with you wherever you go." Bill has been bold and the *Urban Impact* story you just read proves that.

When I think of Bill's faithfulness, I remember his story about telling me to ride my bike after I called to cancel my commitment when my car broke down. That may seem harsh to some, but I needed it. Our work is not a game and our presence can make the difference between life and death. I needed to learn faithfulness and Bill Hobbs is the man to learn it from.

Bill started an outreach that took place every Thursday night for fourteen years. The kids would always ask, "Hey, are you going to Bill's?" and eventually they shortened it to "I'm going to Bill." They had named the Bible study "Bill" because of his faithfulness and presence. Later, I went to a sophisticated youth conference where they told us we had to have a good name that would stick out in the kid's minds and help us market and promote. We had a contest and allowed the kids to name the youth group so they would feel empowered and have buy-in. Do you know what they named it? They came up with B-FAT: Be Faithful, Be Available, Be Teachable. We designed flyers and marketed B-FAT. Six months later, the youth asked,

"Are you going to Bill's FAT?" They still could not disassociate the Bible study from Bill.

I learned something important then. It is not about what's on the outside or the name or how we market what we are doing. It is about what's on the inside—the heart of the organization. Bill has emphasized (and modeled it as well) that we must be faithful if we are going to see any results in the community. I thank Bill for the faithfulness that he has shown throughout his life. I learned my lesson the first time, so when we started an elementary outreach for the younger kids, do you know what I called it? I called it "Little Bill".

When I think of Bill's caring heart, I remember the time he invested in me. We have met for a few hours each week for many years, and it has been a time when Bill listened and prayed for me. He has held me accountable, assigned me books to read, and taken me on educational trips. I told Bill, "I don't think I can plant a church. I don't have this or that skill." Bill replied, "No, you're the man, Chris. I believe you are. I believe in you." Bill believed in me when I didn't believe in myself and today I am a pastor because of his encouragement.

Bill has always carried Psalm 68:5 in his heart: "A father to the fatherless, a defender of widows, is God in his holy dwelling." I have that verse in my heart now because of Bill, and I pray that after reading *Urban Impact: Love, Equip, Empower,* you have it in yours too. We need your help if we are going to build on the legacy Bill has handed us.

I am glad Bill isn't just going away and I am also glad we have had the chance to honor him with a smooth transition, one in which he is still involved in the work he built and loves. This book is titled *Urban Impact*, but it is a story of one man's purpose being lived out through the values and behaviors I described earlier: boldness, faithfulness, and a caring heart. Thank you, Bill, for allowing me to learn from you. I want to continue the work you started in a way that will honor you and bring glory to God. I look forward to many more stories of lives being impacted by this work. God bless you.

Pastor Chris Tress

POSTSCRIPT

As I updated and revised this latest edition of my book, I thought it would be helpful to give you an update on how the COVID-19 pandemic impacted the ministry, our community, and our staff. We were moving forward with many initiatives in March 2020 when suddenly and without warning, the world came to a screeching halt—and we halted with it!

Like everyone else, we were uncertain of what to do or how long the shutdown would last. It was difficult to know if we had the correct information or latest policies or procedures to determine what we could or could not do. The Leadership Academy had to cease after school classes along with the meals we served as part of it and we knew that was not good for the students. We instituted some weekly outreaches where we would drive by homes to connect with the kids, and we were able to distribute some food and water to the families.

We also went online to establish a Google classroom for those kids who did have computers and online capability. We provided academic support and some G Time, which is a devotional time, for them. We got off to a slow start, but we gradually gained momentum and got more people involved.

Our annual gala fundraising event was scheduled for Saturday, March 14, but that of course had to be cancelled. That was early in the pandemic and at first, we were not sure what to do. Eventually, it became clear we had to cancel it along with our golf tournament, which represented a loss of $500,000 of expected revenue.

There was a moment there where we were wondering, *Lord, where do we go from here?* At the same time, we have seen His provision for the ministry since 1997, so we decided to be bold and do what we had never done. We took a huge step of faith and established a $250,000 emergency matching fund. Many of our partners stepped up, which was a humbling experience, as we watched the Lord provide the $250,000.

Then we went out to a broader audience and challenged them to match that amount, which they did. In addition, through the CARES Act, the government provided help for us so we could keep 90% of our staff onboard and employed. We also experimented with an online gala and auction, with which the fundraising department did a fantastic job.

As the pandemic progressed, we had to cancel our summer programming, our annual camping trip, and the Summer Jam, which is a supportive academic program. Then we reengaged slowly as new COVID regulations were announced and began to reach out to the families.

Then when we thought we had an idea of what we could and could not do, tragedy struck again through the murder of George Floyd in Minneapolis. UYI came under fire from some social media attacks questioning our methods and motives over the years in the community. We as an organization had to step back and take a look to evaluate what we were doing and why we were doing it. What are our motives? How do we do a better job at building bridges?

Rather than contributing to the polarization, we

wanted to bring in a spirit that said, "We're listening, learning, and loving." We wanted to draw from and build on our 23 years of experience and the credibility we had to be a voice that would continue to love, equip, and empower inner city youth to fulfill their God-given purpose. We hope to do a better job of rallying, motivating, and empowering the body of Christ to go into their underserved communities and build relationships that can make an impact for healing and wholeness. Our desire is to coach and encourage the churches here and abroad to be able to do that.

At the same time, we had to face a societal issue that we have been facing for decades, and that is the reality of racism and inequalities in our culture and institutions. I have been exposed to racism over the years as I worked with our inner-city youth. For example, one of our young men came to me years ago and said, "Mr. Bill, I got pulled over by the police because they said I ran a stop sign on my bicycle." Unfortunately, his family had been in some trouble with the law, but he had not. We tried to help him walk through and process that event.

I've also been to court with young men accused of minor crimes who had no defense because they had a poor public defender. I saw them receiving sentences beyond the severity of the crime. In one instance, the police showed up at the office and said, "We need to arrest one of the young men you have working here." I said, "Look, you don't need to come into the building. Let's go outside and talk about it" which we did.

They arrested him for selling cocaine to an undercover agent, and they had it on tape. I said to our staff member, "We'll work with you. We're with you and will support you." To make a long story short, we got a lawyer, and the police department could never come up with the evidence. It was a scam. They profiled him but they had no evidence of any crime on his part ever happening. Another young woman who worked with us was pulled over by police who said she was driving her car too close to their police car. They intimidated her a bit but then let her go. She was of course frightened.

Those examples and many others made racial profiling real and close to my world. When people see those situations, their eyes are opened and they think, *My gosh. I didn't realize that it really happened.* We've been fighting this battle by being faithful and building relationships in the community. The color issue in so many ways has been diminished because the community has seen the commitment we've made to their kids. They know of our faithfulness to serve and they understand that UYI is here long term. We're not just here on a three-year grant to make money.

Today, when we look at the issues that are prevalent in America right now, I see that in many cases, we have put a band aid on cancer. We've tried to solve our racial divide and inequity through political reasoning and programming, but we need to sit and then listen, learn, and love. Those practices in themselves bring reconciliation to and empathy for a community that's been underserved, manipulated, and many times profiled in a wrong way.

The George Floyd incident and other deaths that have sparked such outrage caused me personally to stop and check the motives of my own heart. *What is God calling me to do? What is he calling us as an organization to do?* It has caused me to be quiet and wait. I decided to stop talking and start listening more proactively. We know that the Lord uses difficult things, as we are told in James' epistle, to develop perseverance, character, and endurance. I've seen myself grow in places where I am dealing with the heart matters in me that God has exposed.

God help us see the reality of racism and then give us the courage and strength to uproot it from our society, our world, and in ourselves. I believe this starts with the words David penned in Psalm 139:13-14: "For you created my inmost being; you knit me together in my mother's womb. I praise you because I am fearfully and wonderfully made; your works are wonderful; I know that full well." Those verses are true for *every* human being. We are *all* part of God's creation made in his image and likeness. It breaks our Father's heart to see the senseless shooting, violence, and hatred within His creation.

To be part of the solution, we must each start by taking a look in the mirror and examining our hearts. I have asked myself during this season if there is racism in my heart. That question is consistent with David's prayer found later in Psalm 139:23-24: "Search me, God, and know my heart; test me and know my anxious thoughts. See if there is any offensive way in me and lead me in the way everlasting."

God has answered that prayer many times by showing me my offensive ways and the reality of my heart. When he did, I needed to confess my failure, repent, and turn from it and then take action that corrects my fault and honors Him. What about you? Are you willing to let God show you your offensive ways, to confess and repent and then allow Him to make you part of the healing presence in our communities?

I am confident God is using this unrest to wake His people up. I feel strong and focused moving forward. I had gone through some surgery in June 2020, which was another physical setback and break in my schedule which I had to endure along with the pandemic. The reality is that God's hand is upon UYI and each one of our team—including me. I feel like we've grown through the difficulties and I am ready for the next season.

UYI's solution to the problem of racism is that we need to love, equip, and empower now more than ever. We have continued to build bridges with those in the community despite the events of the last eight months. We're going to come out of this better, stronger, and more focused than ever. Building relationships and breaking down walls have taken a long time and are not easy to do, but after 23 years, I think we've been able to be and build a bridge that honors the Lord and loves people where they're at.

When a ministry is involved in cross-cultural work like we are, we must learn that language, customs, and culture mean one thing to one group, but they represent something totally different to another group. There's an awkwardness of learning because sometimes we unintentionally say or do the wrong thing. That word, or phrase, or action would not be thought of in one setting as anything controversial or offensive, but in another setting or for another people group, it can be volatile. What we do is exacting work and this year has made it even more exacting work—and social media has added to that.

When people post things on social media, it's not always verified. it can also be highly subjective as the person posting can add his or her editorial slant to the mix. If it's negative or confirms someone's suspicions of the worst, it can be immediately received as another example of a wrong being done. That requires us to have bigger and better teams in which people are speaking freely to help us all see things from the perspective of those being wronged or offended.

Prior to the pandemic our team had been having much deeper and more honest discussion about race and racial reconciliation, asking exactly what we are representing to the community. We decided we are not in this community to defend or react. We're here to love, equip, and empower. We are here to listen, learn, and love the community right where they are at, humbly accepting that we don't have it all together. We are not going to play verbal volleyball or accusations going back and forth. That's a waste of time.

We have also come to see in this season that it is important to define what exactly we consider success for the work we do. Is it justice? Equality? Freedom? For me at least, my goal has always been healing and reconciliation. I want to help alleviate the pain the inner-city youth are in due to a myriad of social ills. There's one race, the human race, and that was right from our origins with Adam and Eve. Obviously, there's ethnic differences and culture, but there's one race, one Father, one God. Through our sinfulness and fallenness, we created racism.

As I close once again, one of the things that the team has looked at over the years is how do we do a better job reaching the needs of the urban community through education. We desired to have access to the students even earlier in their academic career to keep them from getting so far behind in their basic learning skills.

With that objective in mind, Chris and the team, with my support, took a step in August 2020 and opened Carver Christian Academy with kindergarten classes. Yet again, God provided for everything we needed. As of September 2020, we have twelve kindergarten students who make up our first-ever class. We've had other Christian schools come alongside us and commit to partner and help us in that. The opening of Carver Christian Academy is our statement of where we are heading with the future of Urban Youth Impact. We are here for the long haul and want to expand our services to other local neighborhoods and mobilize the body of Christ to reach these underserved communities with the love of Christ.

ENDNOTES

[1] Oswald Chambers, "Beware of Criticizing Others," in *My Utmost for His Highest* (Grand Rapids: Discovery House Publishers, 1992), July 17th entry.

[2] Chambers, "Fellowship in the Gospel," in *My Utmost for His Highest*, November 10th entry.

[3] L.B. Cowman, *Streams in the Desert* (Uhrichsville, Ohio: Barbour Publishing, Inc., 1965), July 16th entry.

[4] Joshua 24:10 (NLT)

[5] David Blankenhorn, *Fatherless America: Confronting our Most Urgent Social Problem* (New York: BasicBooks, 1995).

[6] Bill Cosby and Dr. Alvin F. Poussaint, *Come on People: On the Path from Victims to Victors* (Nashville: Thomas Nelson, 2007), page 2.

[7] Wess Stafford, *Too Small to Ignore: Why the Least of These Matters Most* (Colorado Springs: WaterBrook Press, 2007), page 177.

[8] Wess Stafford, *Too Small to Ignore: Why the Least of These Matters Most* pages 105-106

[9] Frank Damazio, *The Making of a Leader* (Portland: City Christian Publishing, 1988), page 172.

[10] Damazio, *The Making of a Leader*, page 171.

[11] Cowman, *Streams in the Desert*, June 2nd entry.

[12] Wess Stafford, *Too Small to Ignore: Why the Least of These Matters Most*, page 183.

[13] Henri J. M. Nouwen, *Bread for the Journey: A Daybook of Wisdom and Faith* (New York: HarperOne, 1997), August 19th entry.

CONTACT INFORMATION

Urban Youth Impact
2823 North Australian Avenue
West Palm Beach, FL 33407

Website: www.urbanyouthimpact.com

Email: info@urbanyouthimpact.com
Phone: 561.832.9220
Fax: 561.832.9245

Donations, one-time or recurring gifts, can be made on the website or checks can be sent to:

Urban Youth Impact
P.O. Box 222592
West Palm Beach, FL 33422

Podcast: uyimpact
Instagram: UYImpact
Twitter: UYimpact
Facebook: UYImpact

Urban Youth Impact is a 501©3 non-profit organization. UYI is a certified agency with Nonprofits First (formerly known as the Center for Nonprofit Excellence) and a member of the Combined Federal Campaign, the Christian Community Development Association, and Local Independent Charities of America.

www.ingramcontent.com/pod-product-compliance
Lightning Source LLC
LaVergne TN
LVHW052257070426
835507LV00036B/3265